INDIGENOUS PEOPLES IN
LIBERAL DEMOCRATIC STATES

H. Srikanth

Bäuu Press, Colarado
2010

Copyright © 2010 By H. Srikanth
First Edition

Where used trademarks are acknowledged as the property of their respective owners.

1. Indigenous Peoples - Comparative history. 2. Canada - First Nations. 3. India - Scheduled Tribes. 4. Political sociology.

INDIGENOUS PEOPLES IN LIBERAL DEMOCRATIC STATES
/Author   H. Srikanth
p. cm.
Includes bibliographic references and index.

ISBN 13: 978-0-9820467-4-6

Bäuu Press
PO Box 4445
Boulder, Colorado

INDIGENOUS PEOPLES IN LIBERAL DEMOCRATIC STATES

A Comparative Study of Conflict and Accommodation in Canada and India

H. Srikanth

Bäuu Press, Colarado
2010

Dedicated To

Fr. Joseph Kalicharal
S. Narayana
Shukla Prasad

my school and under-graduate teachers

who introduced me to

the world of life, literature and politics

CONTENTS

ABBREVIATIONS

ADC - Autonomous District Council
ARC - Autonomous Regional Council
AFAs - Alternative Funding Arrangements
AFN - Assembly of First Nations
BC - British Columbia
BCANSI - British Columbia Association of Non-Status-Indians
BCTC - BC Treaty Commission
DIAND - Department of Indian Affairs and Northern Development
FN - First Nations
HBC - Hudson's Bay Company
ILO - International Labor Organization
INAC - Indian and Northern Affairs, Canada
IPACC - Indigenous Peoples of Africa Coordinating Committee
NAIB - North American Indian Brotherhood
NBCC - Native Brotherhood of British Columbia
NCC - National Council of Canada
NDP - New Democratic Party
NEFA - North-East Frontier Agency
NIB - National Indian Brotherhood
NNC - Naga National Council
NSCN (IM) - National Socialist Council of Nagaland – Isak Muivah
NSTFDC - National Scheduled Tribes Finance and Development Corporation
NWC - North West Company
PDS - Public Distribution System
PTGs - Primitive Tribal Groups
PYLL - Potential Years of Life Lost
RCAP - Royal Commission on Aboriginal Peoples
SCs - Scheduled Castes
STs - Scheduled Tribes
SVITF - Southern Vancouver Island Tribal Federation
TRIFED - Tribal Co-Operative Marketing Development Federation of India Ltd.
TSP - Tribal Sub-Plan strategy
UBCIC - Union of British Columbia Indian Chiefs
UNPO - Unrepresented Nations and Peoples Organization
UNWGIP - United Nations' Working Group on Indigenous Populations

LIST OF MAPS AND TABLES

ACKNOWLEDGEMENTS

For over a decade, I have been trying to study and understand the political dynamics of the indigenous peoples inhabiting India's northeastern region. In a way, my interest in tribal politics drove me to apply for Canadian Studies Faculty Research fellowship to study the problems and struggles of First Nations in Canada. My initial commitment under the approved research project entitled, "Liberal Democratic Nations and the Indigenous People: A Comparative Study of the Strategies of Accommodation pursued in the Province of British Columbia in Canada and the State of Assam in India" was only to produce a couple of research papers on the theme and to publish the same in some academic journals in India. But after I started interacting with scholars and activists in Canada and began collecting data from the libraries at the Simon Fraser University and the University of British Columbia, I was so fascinated by the information that I could collect that I decided to write a book. Initially I thought I could complete it in a year or two. But because of my other academic and social preoccupations, it took nearly four years for me to complete the same. As the book is finally getting ready to see the daylight, I cannot but remember all those who assisted me in completing the project.

The book would not have materialized in the first instance, had I not received the Canadian Studies Faculty

Research Fellowship in the year 2005. I am deeply indebted to Shastri Indo-Canadian Institute (SICI) and the International Academic Relations Division of Foreign Affairs, Canada for approving my project proposal and sponsoring my trip to Canada. In Vancouver I was immensely benefited by the discussions I had with John Richards, Professor in Public Policy Program, SFU and Bruce G. Miller, Professor in Anthropology Department at UBC. I am also thankful to Doug McArthur and Jon Kesselman for their guidance and hospitality. The office-bearers of Nuu-Chah-Nulth Tribal Council and Hupacasath First Nation in Vancouver Island allowed me to visit their reserves and helped me in gaining firsthand information about the working of First Nation governments in British Columbia. I am thankful to the library staff of *Xwi7xwa* First Nations Library at UBC. Special gratitude is due to Dr. Moninder Bubber, SICI Liaison librarian, who introduced me to library system in Canadian universities and helped me to get access to necessary books and documents on Canada in SFU libraries.

In India I am deeply indebted to scholars and colleagues like J.B. Bhattacharjee, Sajal Nag and Apurba K. Barua, M. N. Karna and A.C. Sinha who sharpened my knowledge of the peoples of north-east India. By publishing some of my earlier pieces on north-east India in their journals and edited volumes, friends and well-wishers like C.J. Thomas, Girin Phukhan and late Krishna Raj gave me the necessary confidence to undertake this project. I am indebted to North-Eastern Hill University, Shillong for granting me lien for completing the project. I duly acknowledge the services rendered by B.S. Mipun and Ms. Dipsikha of Geography department of NEHU and Mr. Dhiren Bahl of *WordsWay*, New Delhi who helped me in

x

designing the maps and copy editing the draft manuscript. I am also grateful to SICI family in New Delhi - especially Sarmistha Roy, Prachi Kaul and A.S. Narang - for their encouragement and support.

After completing the manuscript, I was looking for a publisher who could ensure that my book reaches the intended target groups – the scholars, academicians, activists and policy-makers - who are concerned about the plight of the indigenous peoples across the world. I am happy that the Bauu Institute and Publishers, engaged in activist research on the indigenous peoples, has come forward to publish my manuscript. I am indeed thankful to Peter N. Jones and his team at the Bauu Institute for their cooperation and hard-work in bringing out the book in the present form.

Finally I do acknowledge that I could not have completed the project, had I not got relief from routine duties at home. I recognize and appreciate the patience and understanding that my wife, Mala and my daughter, Sameera, showed during this period, when I virtually neglected my domestic responsibilities as a husband and father.

I hope the book, which I could finally complete with the encouragement and cooperation of so many kind-hearted people, would be able to receive attention of scholars, activists and policy-makers working for development of the indigenous peoples in different countries.

H. Srikanth

1

INTRODUCTION

W hen colonialism was making inroads into the con-
tinents and countries little known to Europeans at
large, both apologists and critics of colonialism in the West
contended that the indigenous peoples inhabiting the
colonies and semi-colonies would perish as communities
unless they learned to adapt themselves to the changing
times.[1] It was then assumed that penetration of the market
economy, expansion of the institutions of private property,
development of modern education, spread of Christianity,
and growth of liberal values and practices in the colonized
world would overshadow and replace the pre-capitalist
structures and traditions of the native communities and sub-
sume them under the capitalist mainstream. Such predic-
tions, however, did not come true.

　　Despite all the hardships and sufferings that they
had to encounter, the indigenous peoples survived the on-
slaughts of colonialism and made their presence felt in the
post-war world by leading many a struggle for recognition
and restoration of their aboriginal identities and rights. Far
from giving up their identities, the indigenous peoples are
reorganizing themselves as communities and fighting for
restoration of their dignity and rights as indigenous peoples.
Through organized struggles and campaigns at national and
global levels, the indigenous peoples successfully indicted
the colonial rule and were able to internationalize their
problems and concerns. Collectively, they ensured that the

Working Group on Indigenous Populations (WGIP) came out with a Draft Declaration on the Rights of Indigenous Peoples in 1994. In 1995, the Commission on Human Rights established its own working group to examine the Draft Declaration. Although the draft is yet to be adopted by the UN General Assembly, several rounds of negotiations by UNHRC on the draft have helped in influencing the national policies of several countries around the world. Several nation states have revised their earlier policies toward the indigenous peoples and are exploring ways and means to accommodate the interests and concerns of these hitherto neglected and discriminated segments of modern nation states. Compelled to address the indigenous peoples' demands, even powerful liberal democratic states are now amending their constitutions, restructuring their political and administrative structures, reviewing their development strategies and becoming advocates of communitarianism and multiculturalism. However, given the structural limitations of capitalist societies it is not clear at the moment as to what extent the liberal democratic states will be able to fulfill the aspirations of indigenous peoples and succeed in erasing the bitter memories of the colonial past. Assessment of the indigenous peoples' future in modern liberal democratic states requires an understanding of the indigenous peoples' experiences, problems, concerns, aspirations, potentialities, and limitations.

Who are Indigenous Peoples?

The term "indigenous peoples" means different things to different people. Although intellectuals and activists have been debating issues concerning indigenous peoples, they have not yet arrived at one acceptable definition. Both the concept and theory of indigenous peoples are still evolving.

In the Report for the UN Sub-Commission on the Prevention of Discrimination of Minorities (1986), Martinéz Cobo stated that indigenous populations are:

> composed of the existing descendants of the peoples who inhabited the present territory of a country wholly or partially at the time when persons of a different culture or ethnic origin arrived there from other parts of the world, overcame them, by conquest, settlement or other means, reduced them to a non-dominant or colonial condition; who today live more in conformity with their particular social, economic and cultural customs and traditions than with the institutions of the country of which they now form part, under a state structure which incorporates mainly national, social and cultural characteristics of other segments of the population which are predominant.[2]

Cobo's definition is criticized for being limited in scope and focus, as it basically talks about the native aboriginal communities inhabiting the Americas and Oceania and ignores many other deprived tribal and ethnic communities living in other parts of the globe. The International Labor Organization (ILO) in its Convention No. 169 on the working rights of Indigenous and Tribal Peoples, 1989, used the said term to refer to both tribal peoples whose social, cultural, and economic conditions distinguish them from other sections of the national community and whose status is regulated wholly or partially by their own customs or traditions or by special laws or regulations, and also to peoples who are regarded as indigenous on account of their descent from the populations which inhabited the country at the time of conquest or colonization.[3] Realizing that there are several communities in the world claiming indigenous status on one or the other grounds, Erica-Irene Daes, Chairperson of UNWGIP, avoided giving a precise definition of the term. Yet she helped in broadening the concept by recognizing different communities of peoples as indigenous. According to her, indigenous peoples include: (1) descendants of groups which were in the territory of the country at the time when other groups of different cultures or ethnic origins arrived there; (2) those who have preserved almost intact the customs and traditions of their ancestors which are similar to those characterized as indigenous because of their isolation from other segments of the country's population; and (3) those who are placed under a state structure which incorporates national, social, and cultural characteristics alien to theirs.[4] The Indigenous Peoples of Africa Co-ordinating Committee (IPACC), which articulates the indigenous claims in Africa, argued that the concept should encompass all politically and economically marginalized people in colonial set-ups; communities such as the San and the Pygmy who are physically distinct and hence subject to specific forms of discrimination and, those hunting and herding people who inhabit deserts and forests and are discriminated against and dominated by agricultural peoples in the state system.[5] Realizing the changing contours of the concept, even the World Bank has given directives to identify the indigenous peoples on the bases of the following characteristics: (1) close attachment to ancestral territories and to the natural resources in those areas; (2) self-identification and identification by others as members of a distinct cultural group; (3) an indigenous language, often different from the national language; (4) presence of customary social and political institutions; and (5) primarily subsistence-oriented production.[6]

In the background of all such efforts to understand and respond to the issues of indigenous people, the term indigenous people has been gaining popularity among aboriginal peoples inhabiting developed countries like Canada in recent decades. However, ever since their territories were colonized, the Native Indian communities in Canada, who now call themselves First Nations, have been fighting for recognition and restoration of their identities and rights as aboriginal peoples/First People. As was evident in the reports of the Royal Commission to Sieur de Monts (1603) and the British Royal Proclamation of 1763, the French and British colonizers had recognized the aboriginal Indians of Canada as indigenous nations and stressed the need for entering into mutually beneficial treaties with them. Although in subsequent decades the treaties became unequal and one-sided, still treaties continued to be viewed as the basis of the aboriginal – Canadian relations. The native activists and organizations in Canada view their fight for recognition of their separate identities and interests as aboriginal peoples as part of the global struggles of the indigenous peoples. But this has not been the case in India, wherein the British colonizers annexed both tribal and non-tribal territories and made everyone the subjects of British India. Although certain legal immunities were given to certain categories of backward communities, who were later recognized as scheduled tribes, the British did not officially treat them as indigenous nations. The colonial power granted some concessions to certain tribal communities and regions in India, not because the tribes were recognized as indigenous nations, but because they were treated as backward communities needing state protection. Partly influenced by this colonial precedent, the post-colonial rulers in India also refused to give official recognition to tribal communities as indigenous people. This reason apart, the national leadership in India consciously avoided acknowledging the idea of indigenous people considering the fact that the Indian subcontinent has been host to hundreds of immigrant communities, tribal and non-tribal. Unlike the European colonizers, the early immigrants who migrated to India at different points of time settled in India and made it their homeland. They integrated themselves with the communities which were already there and contributed in their own ways to the development of Indian civilization. Since the communities moved from one part of the country to another it is difficult to know for sure who among the communities came and settled first in the territories of their present habitation. Although the local expression *adivasi* (meaning the "first people") is used in India to refer to tribes, to call all tribes "first peoples" or "first settlers" is beset with many problems. Many non-tribal communities like the Ahoms and Koch living in India today were also tribes at one time. Further, some tribes such as the Kukis in northeast India migrated to the present areas of their habitation only during the British rule.[7] Prior to British colonization India was more a geographical and civilizational entity than a unified political unit. The possibilities of building nation states in such multicultural and multiethnic countries developed only after the European colonizers annexed the territories inhabited by different communities and brought them under a common colonial political and administrative structure. The contradictions of colonial rule gave birth to anti-colonial movements led by the emerging national bourgeoisie. After gaining political independence the new ruling elite in the post-colonial states took upon themselves the tortuous task of building modern nation states by bringing together various communities of people belonging to different races, languages, religions, and nationalities. Any official acceptance of the chronological definition of indigenous peoples in such states engaged in nation building would create politically explosive situations, threatening their nation-building projects. In view of all these considerations, Indian intellectuals like Andre Beteille, Justice Y. K. Sabharwal, and others expressed their reservations against the use of the term "indigenous peoples" in the Indian context.[8]

Notwithstanding such objections, one comes across many activists and social scientists in India who think that it is appropriate to designate Scheduled Tribes (STs) in the country as indigenous peoples.[9] According to them the tribes are indigenous peoples, not because they are the first settlers, but because they have many things in common in normative and relational senses with indigenous peoples of the Americas and Oceania. Arguing their case, about 20 social scientists who gathered at the Indian Institute of Advanced Study, Shimla, in 1993 stated in their resolution that:

> the word "indigenous" should be used not in [the] chronological sense but in the normative sense to cover people who feel rooted in their surroundings, entertain a custodial sense about their territory and resources, are bound together primarily through moral bindings and entertain a sense of reciprocity and mutuality reinforced by egalitarian ethos. We consider that in [the] ideal typical cognitive realm, tribe as a social category can be considered to be indigenous in the foregoing sense.[10]

According to this perspective indigenous peoples are distinguished by their continuing adherence to traditional ways of life, their wish to maintain their aboriginal identities, and their opposition to all external attempts at mainstreaming them. Communities are identified as indigenous on the basis of the kind of relationship they have with the dominant communities that hold political and economic power in the nation states. Colonization of traditional lands and resources, cultural subordination and racial discrimination, structural incapability to compete with dominant communities in a competitive market economy, inferior socioeconomic status, denial of the right to self-determination, etc. are the bases for identifying indigenous peoples. Invoking similar logic, some tribal communities in India are asserting their status as indigenous and making efforts to build alliances with other similar communities elsewhere. The Isaac–Muivah faction of the National Socialist Council of Nagaland (NSCN–IM), for example, has ensured international recognition of the Nagas as an indigenous people by becoming a member of the Unrepresented Nations and Peoples Organization (UNPO). Several global organizations working for the cause of indigenous peoples have also given recognition to STs as indigenous peoples and are providing moral support to their struggles.

The meaning and scope of the term indigenous people has thus evolved over time. Initially, it was used to refer to the communities that inhabited the Americas and Oceania prior to European colonization. But of late as a result of active interventions and rigorous campaigning by different NGOs in Asia and Africa, many other peripheral and subjugated communities in post-colonial societies have also started getting recognition as indigenous peoples. In the present context, the categories of people who are accepted as indigenous peoples include the following:

H. SRIKANTH

1. Descendants of groups of people who inhabited the territories prior to the arrival of other groups of people who were culturally different and economically and politically more powerful.

2. Communities of people who lived in isolation, practicing their own customs and traditions before they were conquered and subjected to alien control and exploitation.

3. Tribal communities that are bound together through sense of reciprocity and mutuality, reinforced by egalitarian ethos emanating from their predominantly non-acquisitive material existence.

4. Marginalized ethnic communities that, despite their peripheral status in colonial and post-colonial societies, refuse to be assimilated into the dominant national culture.

5. Socially and politically backward communities that mostly depend on traditional occupations which have little relevance to a market-oriented capitalist economy.

Need to Study Indigenous Peoples

These conceptual and theoretical developments enable us to understand several communities spread across the world as indigenous peoples. The term "indigenous peoples" now covers a wide range of communities starting from the Aboriginal First Nations (FNs), Inuit, and Metis in Canada to the Samis in Scandinavia, Maoris in New Zealand, Pygmies in Uganda to the STs in India. The identification of communities or peoples as indigenous is a two-way process. At one level the communities are identifying themselves as indigenous peoples and bonding with other indigenous communities in national and global arenas to defend their rights. At another level, irrespective of whether the particular national governments recognize them that way or not, the global community is according recognition to them as indigenous peoples and lending their support to the struggles of aboriginal peoples. With several indigenous peoples' struggles now receiving global attention thanks to media attention and the growing concern for human rights, several activist NGOs and intellectuals in different disciplines across the globe have started documenting various issues concerning them. A number of insightful documents, research articles and books have been written and published on their problems and struggles in different countries. Some such studies have also probed the responses of national governments.

However, there are not many comparative studies analyzing the indigenous peoples' struggles in different countries.[11] Most have focused on the native people's struggles in North America and Oceania. One hardly comes across studies comparing the indigenous peoples' experiences and movements in developed and developing countries. These would help in broadening our understanding of indigenous peoples in different stages of development. They would also widen our knowledge of how modern states with different socio-cultural milieus handle the challenges posed by the indigenous peoples' movements. Since each state is experimenting in its own ways to accommodate the indigenous peoples, there is a lot one could gain from each others' experiences. The present book, written primarily with these objectives, seeks to comprehend the interface between the state and the indigenous peoples in two countries, namely, Canada and India. In the background of the experiences of FNs in Canada and the STs in India, the book investigates the extent to which the two countries – claiming to be liberal parliamentarian democracies, but at different stages of capitalist development – have

H. SRIKANTH

been able to uphold the interests and concerns of the indigenous peoples in their respective countries. To contextualize the concerns of the book, one may start with a general understanding of the history, struggles, and present status of the FNs in Canada and the STs in India.

Aboriginal First Nations in Canada

The Constitution Act of 1982 recognizes FNs, Metis, and Inuit as the aboriginal peoples of Canada. The total aboriginal population in Canada was 976,305 in 2001. They account for only 3.3 percent of the total population of Canada. FN people, who are officially referred to as Native Indians, constitute about 65 percent of the total aboriginal population in Canada. Nearly 60 percent of FNs live on reserves.[12] The distribution of the FN populations across Canada is shown in Map 1. Following the colonization of North America, these indigenous communities lost aboriginal rights over their territories and were confined to living on reserves. FNs experienced racial and discriminatory policies for about one hundred years. The Canadian government denied their identities and rights as aboriginal peoples on one hand and on the other refused to treat them as Canadian citizens.[13] Despite all these obstacles that they experienced under colonial and Canadian regimes, FNs in Canada began to organize themselves into different associations and fight for their identity and rights as aboriginal peoples. Participation and positive contribution of FNs to the Allies in the Second World War helped Canadian citizens overcome their racist bias and compelled the government to give up its oppressive and discriminatory policies and attitudes towards the aboriginal peoples. The Canadian government guaranteed citizenship rights to FNs and allowed them to participate in federal and provincial elections. Since the

1950s, the Canadian state has been taking definite steps to bridge the socioeconomic disparities between the aboriginal and non-aboriginal communities.

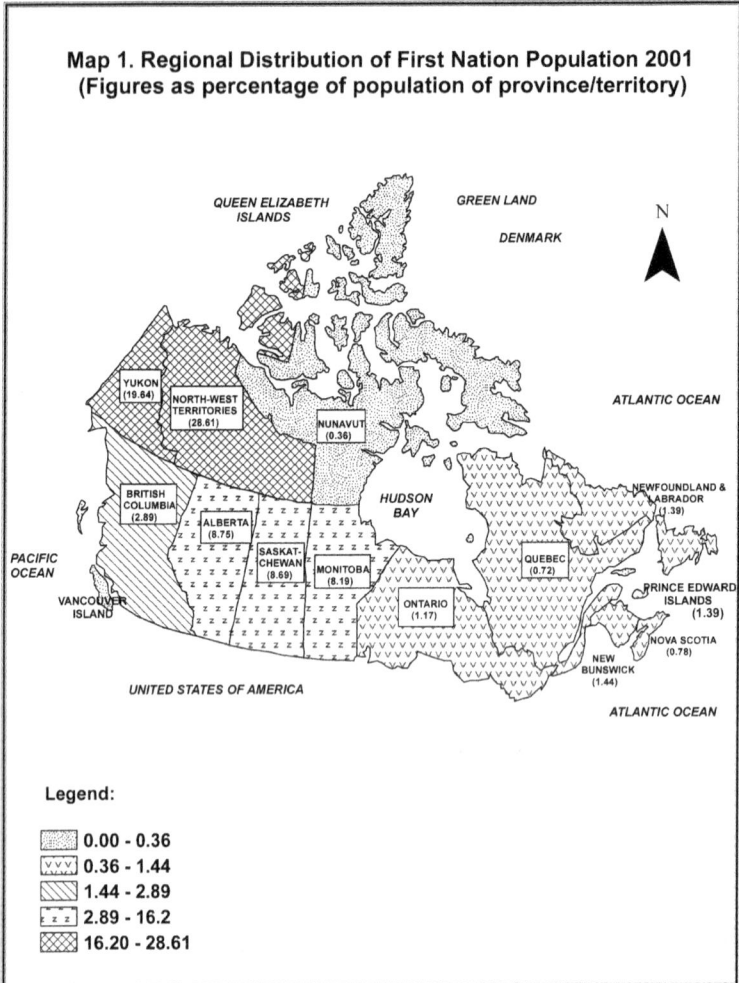

**Map 1. Regional Distribution of First Nation Population 2001
(Figures as percentage of population of province/territory)**

QUEEN ELIZABETH ISLANDS

GREEN LAND

DENMARK

N

YUKON (19.64)

NORTH-WEST TERRITORIES (28.61)

NUNAVUT (0.36)

ATLANTIC OCEAN

BRITISH COLUMBIA (2.89)

ALBERTA (6.75)

SASKAT-CHEWAN (8.69)

MONITOBA (8.19)

HUDSON BAY

NEWFOUNDLAND & LABRADOR (1.39)

PACIFIC OCEAN

QUEBEC (0.72)

VANCOUVER ISLAND

ONTARIO (1.17)

PRINCE EDWARD ISLANDS (1.39)

NOVA SCOTIA (0.78)

NEW BUNSWICK (1.44)

UNITED STATES OF AMERICA

ATLANTIC OCEAN

Legend:

0.00 - 0.36
0.36 - 1.44
1.44 - 2.89
2.89 - 16.2
16.20 - 28.61

Although the living conditions of FNs have improved over the years, income disparities between the FN communities and the rest of the Canadian population continue.[14] Even to this day, the majority of FN individuals are preoccupied in traditional sectors and employed in primary and unskilled jobs. Not many have access to higher education. They are underrepresented in managerial and white-collar jobs. The unemployment rate remains the highest among FNs. Although their health indicators have improved to some extent, FNs continue to top the list of incidence for tuberculosis, alcoholism, drug addiction, suicide, and Potential Years of Life Lost due to injury. Although they have been granted citizenship rights, one hardly finds aboriginal representation in the parliament, assemblies and ministries at federal and provincial governments. To this day there is no province in Canada wherein aboriginal peoples are in a majority. Regions like the Northwest Territories, Yukon Territory, and Nunavut, which have substantial aboriginal populations, do not enjoy the status of provinces. Till the 1970s many of the policies and programs for FNs were executed by Canadian governments without involving the band members. Since the band governments constituted under the Indian Act neither had administrative powers nor financial resources to conceive and implement programs of their choice, they failed to satisfy the natives' urge for autonomy and self-reliance. For decades the FN communities in Canada have been waging relentless struggles for self-governments conceived and administered by the FNs themselves. It is only in recent decades that their movements began to bear fruit with the Canadian governments' recognition of aboriginal peoples' right to self-government.

Status of Scheduled Tribes in India

Like the FNs in Canada, STs in India are a legally-notified category. Officially, all STs are tribes, but all those which claim themselves to be tribes may not be STs. Only those communities which have been declared as such by the President of India through a gazette notification or through an amendment of the Act of Parliament will be considered STs. Over the years the Government of India has included several communities in the list of STs. According to the Annual Report 2004–05 of the Ministry of Tribal Affairs, 700 communities are notified as STs. The total population of STs in 2001 was 84.3 million, constituting 8.2 percent of the total population of the country. The ST population grew at a rate of 24.45 percent during the period 1991–2001. The STs are spread over 187 tribal districts covering an area of 0.4 million sq km. Some, like the Bhils, Gonds, Santhals, Meenas, and so forth number in the millions, whereas others like the Chimals and Jarawas in the Andaman & Nicobar Islands are reported to be less than a hundred. Most STs live in central India, although numerically they are not in a majority in any of the states there. Interestingly, although the tribal people in the seven northeastern states together constitute only about 12 percent of the total ST population in the country, they constitute the majority in four states. Map 2 shows state-wise distribution of STs in India.

In general the tribal communities in India had experienced the worst forms of exploitation, oppression, discrimination and alienation during the British rule. Because of their socioeconomic backwardness the STs could not cope with the changes introduced by the colonial regime. Colonial developments like the introduction of private property relations, penetration of markets, takeover of forests, imposition of taxes, and restrictions imposed on shifting cultivation worsened the plight of the tribal communities. Taking note of the sad state of tribal communities, after India became independent, the post-colonial regime took several initiatives to improve the living

Map 2. State-wise Distribution of Scheduled Tribe Population in India 2001 (Figures as percentage of state population)

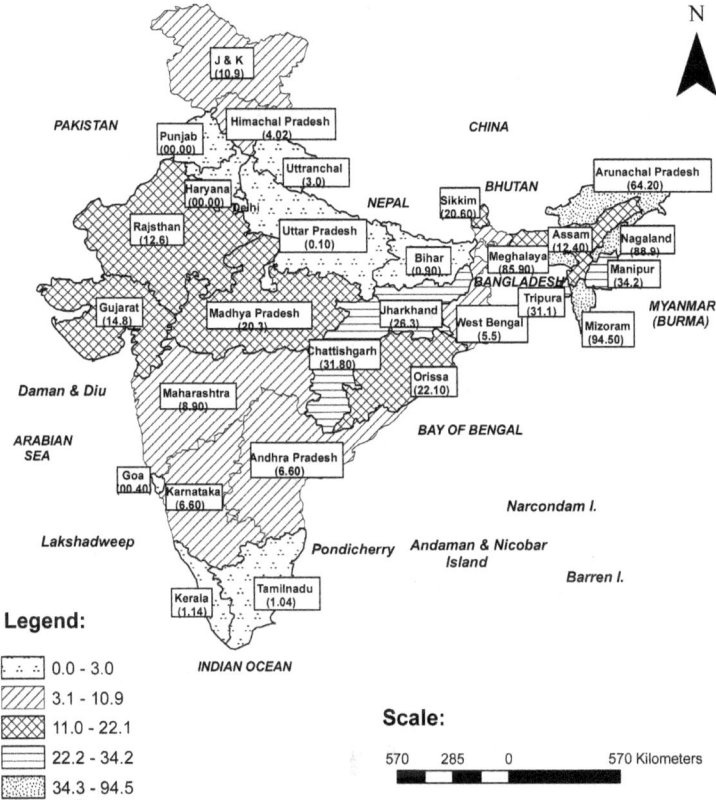

N

Region	Percentage
J & K	(10.9)
PAKISTAN	
Punjab	(00.00)
Himachal Pradesh	(4.02)
CHINA	
Uttranchal	(3.0)
Arunachal Pradesh	(64.20)
Haryana	(00.00)
Delhi	
NEPAL	
BHUTAN	
Sikkim	(20.60)
Rajsthan	(12.6)
Uttar Pradesh	(0.10)
Assam	(12.40)
Nagaland	(88.9)
Bihar	(0.90)
Meghalaya	(85.90)
Manipur	(34.2)
BANGLADESH	
Gujarat	(14.8)
Madhya Pradesh	(20.3)
Jharkhand	(26.3)
West Bengal	(5.5)
Tripura	(31.1)
MYANMAR (BURMA)	
Mizoram	(94.50)
Chattishgarh	(31.80)
Orissa	(22.10)
Daman & Diu	
Maharashtra	(8.90)
ARABIAN SEA	
BAY OF BENGAL	
Goa	(00.40)
Karnataka	(6.60)
Andhra Pradesh	(6.60)
Narcondam I.	
Lakshadweep	
Pondicherry	
Andaman & Nicobar Island	
Barren I.	
Kerala	(1.14)
Tamilnadu	(1.04)

Legend:

- 0.0 - 3.0   INDIAN OCEAN
- 3.1 - 10.9
- 11.0 - 22.1   **Scale:**
- 22.2 - 34.2   570   285   0   570 Kilometers
- 34.3 - 94.5

Source:Census of India, 2001, Government of India

conditions of the tribal communities. Furthermore, the Constitution of India made special provisions for the development of STs. Under Schedules V and VI of the Constitution some degree of autonomy was granted to tribal areas for administering their own affairs. Several Acts, programs and policies have been initiated to protect and promote the socioeconomic status of the tribal peoples. In 1999 a separate Ministry of Tribal Welfare was constituted at the Center with the objective of ensuring integrated socioeconomic development of the tribal communities.

The constitutional safeguards and the governments' interventions no doubt did help in bringing about marginal changes in the lives of STs. But even today there are any number of tribal villages in India that lack basic facilities like roads, electricity, safe drinking water, schools and health-care centers, communication facilities and an effective Public Distribution System (PDS). The governments' policy of affirmative action did help a small section of tribal people to climb the political and administrative ladders and attain middle-class status. However, such privileged sections, often referred to as the tribal elite, constitute a very small fraction of the tribal population. The majority of STs, especially those living in the villages and interiors, still suffer from different types of deprivation. Many amongst them continue to live in inhospitable terrains like forests or hilly areas. The tribals gained little even in the regions which witnessed rapid economic development. The industries that came up in the tribal areas hardly employ the tribal people. Although most of the dams are located in tribal areas the percentage of irrigated tribal landholdings remained far below the percentage of irrigated landholdings of the general population. Many development initiatives like construction of dams, power projects, roads, airports, industries, etc. have displaced over one million tribal people from their original habitats. Many landless tribal laborers and displaced tribal people migrate to urban areas to eke out a living by working as coolies or casual laborers in mines and industries.[15]

The STs lag behind the general population in all human development indicators such as literacy, health, employment, and income. The majority of them are engaged in the primary sector. A large number of tribes continue to practice dry cultivation in the plain areas and shifting cultivation in the hills or forests. Because of constraints imposed by poverty, indebtedness, primitive technologies, unfriendly market conditions, and lack of access to irrigation and power, most tribal people find it difficult to carry on cultivation. They tend to sell their lands to those better-off among the tribal communities or lease their lands to enterprising non-tribal peasants. Many Primitive Tribal Groups (PTGs) eke out their living depending on their traditional occupations such as hunting, rearing animals, handicrafts and tool-making. Despite provision for reservation in education and jobs, the tribals who could make it to higher education and to white-collar and managerial jobs are still few.[16]

The deprivations that tribal peoples in India encounter are in several respects similar to those of the FNs in Canada. Awareness of their status and their distinct identities has given birth to different kinds of tribal movements in India. The tribals have participated in different radical movements led by the leftist parties against feudal and capitalist exploitation. Besides, the tribals themselves have led many movements against the domination of non-tribals in different parts of the country. Several social movements for restoration of tribal institutions, culture, language, and traditions have taken place. The feeling that they cannot have a future in governments led by the non-tribal elite has given birth to different types of autonomy movements for self-rule. Compelled by growing tribal militancy the Government of India had to reorient the forest and other development policies which had colonial overtones. New autonomous district councils and new states had to be created to accommodate the tribals' aspirations for self-rule. It is, however, not yet clear whether the new political arrangements conceded by the governments in response to the tribal movements will really ensure political autonomy and economic development of the STs in India.

Scope and Structure of the Book

An overview of the status of FNs in Canada and STs in India indicates that despite some positive changes that have taken place in the recent past, the indigenous peoples continue to remain peripheral to the politics and economies of the countries they live in. But such apparent similarities should not let one ignore regional- and community-specific differences. One can see differences not only across the countries, but within each of the countries. A study of a general nature is likely to miss the specificities and particularities of indigenous experiences. For an in-depth understanding of the colonial and post-colonial influences, it is necessary to focus on one region in each country and to make an in-depth study of the interface between the indigenous peoples and the governments in those specific regions. Taking this viewpoint, the book confines its scope to the study of the on-reserve FN in the province of British Columbia in Canada and to indigenous tribal communities inhabiting the hill areas of composite Assam in India.

British Columbia is the westernmost of Canada's provinces. It is bordered by the Pacific Ocean on the west, by the US state of Alaska on the northwest, on the north by the Yukon and the Northwest Territories, on the east by the province of Alberta, and on the south by the US states of Washington, Idaho, and Montana. For centuries these territories were inhabited by different indigenous communities. According to some estimates, the total population of the indigenous peoples inhabiting BC at the time

H. SRIKANTH

of the European contact was half the total of the aboriginal population of present-day Canada. British adventurers and traders explored the region only in the nineteenth century. The Hudson's Bay Company (HBC) and the North West Company (NWC), trading in fur, established their settlements in the region for the purpose of trade. In order to compete with the Americans, the two companies united into one in 1821 and took the charter and name of Hudson's Bay Company. Till the mid-nineteenth century the territory was managed by the company. But the bullying tactics of the US government and the immigration of many Americans to BC in search of gold compelled the British government to take direct charge of the mainland territory in 1858, naming it British Columbia. In 1866 Vancouver Island merged with the province of BC. After the formation of the Canadian federation, BC joined it in 1871.

Today BC is one of the most developed provinces of Canada. It has a resource-dominated economy centered on forestry, industry, and mining. Film production and marijuana cultivation also contribute considerably to the provincial economy. Its GDP in 2001 was $190,214 million. Only 4.5 percent of the working population is unemployed in the province as against the Canadian average of 6.2 percent. Its population in 2008 was over 4.4 million. British Columbia is a multicultural province with a considerable migrant population from Asian and European countries.

In contrast, the hill areas of composite Assam that the book intends to study is not a province or state of post-colonial India. By composite Assam, we refer to the territories earlier under the control of the Commissionership of Assam under British rule in the nineteenth century. In addition to the plains of the Brahmaputra and Surma valleys, composite Assam comprises different hill districts and frontier tracts. The hill areas of the princely states of Manipur and Tripura were not part of composite Assam. The political map of composite Assam underwent considerable changes in the twentieth century. After Assam became a Governor's province in 1921, the North-Eastern Frontier Tracts were separated from the direct control of Assam and left almost unadministered. On the eve of India's independence, Assam state had retained control over all other hill districts. But subsequently, partly because of indigenous people's movements and partly for administrative reasons, most hill districts of composite Assam were separated from the state of Assam. Today there are only two hill districts in Assam, Karbi-Anglong and North Cachar Hills. Other tribal-dominant hill districts/tracts have now become separate states of Arunachal Pradesh, Meghalaya, Mizoram, and Nagaland. Irrespective of whether they are autonomous districts of Assam or separate states within the Indian Union, one can look at all these hill districts/tracts together as a region for the following reasons: (1) The indigenous tribal peoples constitute a majority in all these hill areas. (2) They were all subject to British colonial administration in one way or another. (3) Racially and culturally they are very different from the Indians of mainland India. (4) Located in the northeastern region, far away from mainland India, these areas remain underdeveloped and peripheral to the Indian economy. (5) The hills are close to the neighboring countries of Bangladesh, Myanmar, or China, with which they had cultural and trade relations prior to the partition of British India. (6) The indigenous communities in the hills entertain ambivalent relations with the Indian state and mainland Indians to this day. (7) These hill areas are witness to several identity and autonomy movements of the indigenous communities that have changed the political map of northeast India to some extent.

Looked at from the development angle, the two regions have little in common: BC is a developed province in Canada, whereas the hills of composite Assam in northeast India are one of the underdeveloped regions in the country. But historically and socially these two regions have certain similarities. They were the last outposts of British colonization in their respective countries. In both countries, colonization subjugated the native communities and weakened their traditional political institutions. However, the indigenous communities in these two regions did not experience any large-scale displacement like their counterparts living in other parts of their countries. The reserves in BC and the autonomous districts/regions in the hill areas of northeast India were created more or less in areas which the bands/tribes traditionally inhabited. The reserves in BC and the scheduled districts of composite Assam restricted the movements of indigenous communities and prevented their contact with more advanced communities living in their vicinity, but they also helped in preserving the tribal culture and traditions to a considerable extent. The spread of Christianity and modern education influenced the native communities in both countries, but they could not make the tribes give up their tribal identities. In the post-colonial period these indigenous communities led many an uncompromising struggle for autonomy and self-government, asserting their aboriginal identities. The indigenous peoples' struggles in these two regions might not have threatened the political foundations of Canada and India, but they did succeed in forcing the policy makers in the respective countries to acknowledge the aboriginal rights, amend their constitutions, and reorganize their political and economic policies and programs.

These differences and commonalities apparent in the two regions provide sufficient basis for a comparative and analytical study of the indigenous peoples' movements in the two countries. This book seeks to investigate the changing conditions of indigenous peoples in the two regions and explore the nature of the relationship that has been emerging in the two countries between the governments and the indigenous peoples. By undertaking a comparative study of issues, movements, agendas, organizations, and struggles of the native communities and by analyzing the nature of interactions taking place between the governments and indigenous peoples in the two regions, the book aims to grasp the extent to which the liberal democratic states of Canada and India can accommodate the interests and aspirations of the indigenous peoples within the framework of a nation state. Keeping these objectives in mind, Chapters 2 and 3 examine the impact of British colonialism on the FNs in BC and the hill tribes of composite Assam in India and evaluate the state policies toward the indigenous peoples in the two regions till 1950. Chapter 4 examines the indigenous peoples' movements in BC since the 1950s to the beginning of the twenty-first century and throws light on the emerging relations between Canada and the First Nations. Chapter 5 studies the nature of the political institutions and developmental interventions that took place in the hill areas of northeast India since independence and examines their impact on the indigenous tribal communities. Based on the findings of the preceding chapters, the concluding chapter makes a comparative analytical study of the status and struggles of native peoples and the response of the governments to the challenges posed by the indigenous people in Canada and India.

Notes and References

1. Karl Marx and Frederick Engels, *Selected Works, Vol. I* (Moscow: Progress Publishers, 1977), 488–99; David Bedford, "Marxism and the Aboriginal Question: The Tragedy of Progress," *Canadian Journal of Native Studies*14:1 (1994): 101–16; Louis Proyect, "Colonialism, Indigenous Peoples and Split in European Socialism," *Marxism Mailing List Archive*, 26 November 1999, http://archives.econ.utah.edu/archives/marxism/1999w47/msg0020 1.htm accessed 4 July 2008; For arguments of colonial apologists refer, Niall Ferguson, *Empire: How Britain Made the Modern World* (London: Penguin, 2002); Lawrence James, *Raj: The Making and Unmaking of British India* (New York: St Martin's Press, 1999);. A. P. Thornton, *Doctrines of Imperialism* (New York: John Wiley, 1965).

2. Martinez Cobo quoted in "International Day of the World's Indigenous People," Asian Center for the Progress of Peoples, August 2007, http://www.acpp.org/sevents/0809.html accessed 4 July 2008.

3. ILO, *Indigenous and Tribal Peoples and the ILO* (Geneva: International Labour Office, 1994).

4. "Identification of Indigenous Peoples," International Working Group for Indigenous Affairs (IWGIA), http://www.iwgia.org/sw641.asp accessed 10 July 2008.

5. "Who are the Indigenous Peoples of Africa?" IPACC, http://www.ipacc.org.za/eng/who.asp accessed 4 July 2008.

6. World Bank, "World Bank Indigenous Peoples' Operational Directive DD 4.2," July 2005, http://wbln0018.worldbank.org/Institutional/Manuals/OpManual.nsf/tocall/0F7D6F3F04DD70398525672 C007D08ED?OpenDocument accessed 4 July 2008.

7. For a review of the debate, see Virginius Xaxa, "Tribes as Indigenous People of India," *Economic and Political Weekly*, 18 December 1999, 3589–96.

8. Andre Beteille, "The Idea of Indigenous People," *Current Anthropology* 39:2 (1998): 187–91; see also Y. K. Sabharwal's address to the Plenary Session of the International Law Association in Toronto, http://www.supremecourtofindia.nic.in/new_links/ILA-TORONTO.doc accessed 10 July 2008.
9. Andre Beteille objects to calling the tribes indigenous peoples since acceptance of the term would shift the focus from the more compelling problems of tribal development and integration to issues of political power.
10. B. K. Roy Burman, "Indigenous and Tribal Peoples in World System Perspective,", *Studies of Tribes and Tribals* 1:1 (July 2003): 7–27.
11. Refer Noel Dyck, ed., *Indigenous People and the Nation State: Fourth World Politics in Canada, Australia and New Zealand* (St Johns, Newfoundland: Institute of Social and Economic Research, 1985); P. Havemann, ed., *Indigenous Peoples' Rights in Australia, Canada and New Zealand* (Auckland: Oxford University Press, 1999); Duncan Ivison, Paul Patton and Will Sanders, eds., *The Political Theory of Indigenous Peoples* (Cambridge: Cambridge University Press, 2000); Roger L. Nichols, *Indians in the United States and Canada: A Comparative History* (Lincoln: University of Nebraska Press, 1998); Alexander M. Ervin, "Contrasts Between the Resolution of Native Land Claims in the United States and Canada Based on Observations of the Alaska Native Claims Movement," *Canadian Journal of Native Studies* 1:1 (1981): 123–39; Donna Craig, *Indigenous Peoples and Governance Structures: A Comparative Analysis of Land and Resource Management Rights* (Canberra: Aboriginal Studies Press, 2002); Bruce G. Miller, *Invisible Indigenes: The Politics of Non Recognition* (Lincoln: University of Nebraska Press, 2003).
12. The aboriginal population in Canada crossed the one million mark in 2008. The percentage of the FN population living on reserves was reported as 57.2 percent in 2002.
13. Renee Dupius[Author: or "Renée Dupuis"?], *Justice for Canada's Aboriginal Peoples* (Toronto: James Lorimer, 2002), 38–75; Mark Francis, "The 'Civilizing' of Indigenous People in Nineteenth-Century Canada," *Journal of World History* 9:1 (Spring 1998): 51–87.; John L. Tobias, "Protection, Civilization, Assimilation: An Outline History of Canada's Indian Policy," in *As Long as the Sun Shines and the Water Flows*, ed. Ian Getty and Antoina Lussier (Vancouver, UBC Press, 1983), 39-55.

14. Refer *Socio-economic Indicators in Indian Reserves and Comparable Communities, 1971–1991* (Ottawa: DIAND, 1997); Basic Departmental Data 2003 (Ottawa: DIAND, March 2004).
15. For adverse effects of developmental projects on tribal communities, refer Walter Fernandes, ed., *National Development and Tribal Deprivation* (New Delhi: Indian Social Institute, 1992), 1-20; Jagannath Pathy, "Impact of Development Projects on Tribals," in *Tribal Situation in India: Issues in Development*, ed. Vidyut Joshi (New Delhi: Rawat Publications, 1998), 275-284; Joseph Marianus Kujur, "'Development' not for Tribes," http://www.minesandcommunities.org/Country/india17.htm accessed 12 July 2008); Sharad Kulkarni, "The Plight of the Tribal," *Seminar*, 492 (2000), www.india-seminar.com/2000/492/492%20s.%20kulkarni.htm accessed 12 July 2008; Amrita Patwardhan, "Dams and Tribal People in India," paper contributed to the World Commission on Dams, http://www.dams.org/docs/kbase/contrib/soc207.pdf accessed 13 July 2008.
16. Refer "National Health Policy 2001," in *Policy Documents of the Government of India, Compendium I*, compiled by Prakash Louis (New Delhi: Indian Social Institute, 2004), 194-7; see also "National Policy on Tribals, 2003," in *Policy Documents of the Government of India, Compendium II*, compiled by Prakash Louis (New Delhi: Indian Social Institute, 2006), 52-68; Virginius Xaxa, "Positive Discrimination: Why Scheduled Tribes Lag Behind Scheduled Castes?" *Economic and Political Weekly*, 21 July 2001, 2766-72; Planning Commission, *Tenth Five Year Plan, 2002–07*, Vol. 2, Ch. 4.2 http://planningcommission.nic.in/plans/planrel/fiveyr/10th/volume2/v2_ch4_2.pdf accessed 12 July 2008.

H. Srikanth

2

COLONIALISM AND FIRST NATIONS IN BRITISH COLUMBIA

C olonialism has contributed immensely to the development of human progress and civilization. By giving impetus to the development of science, technology, and modern industry and by encouraging hard work, creativity and an adventurous spirit, European colonialism changed the face of the world as never before. Colonization generated enormous wealth and helped the colonial countries to emerge as powerful nation states on the world stage. But these apparently positive developments should not make one overlook the negative impact of colonial rule on indigenous peoples. History shows that wherever the colonizers set foot they destroyed the traditional institutions of governance, exploited the natural resources, and set in motion unintended and unexpected trajectories in the histories of indigenous peoples inhabiting the colonies and semi-colonies. Although the essence of colonialism remains the same everywhere, forms of colonial rule differed from country to country. Based on the extent of immigration and the nature of colonial administration, one can distinguish between two types of colonies: those in the Americas and Oceania where the European immigrants migrated in the hundreds of thousands and settled in the colonies permanently; and others as in India and China where the European immigrants were few and the motive force of the colonizers was not to make the colonies their homelands, but to exploit the people and resources of the colonies for the benefit of their homelands in Europe. Since structures and forms of colonial rule varied, the colonial experiences of indigenous peoples in countries like Canada, the US, Australia, New Zealand, and others differed in many respects from that of countries like India, China, and Egypt. Unless one undertakes an in-depth study of the life-experiences of native communities in different sets of colonies, it is not possible to account for differences in the nature and forms of indigenous peoples' struggles across the world. In pursuit of this objective, an attempt is made in this chapter to throw light on the FN situation in the Canadian province of BC from the time it was colonized to the mid-twentieth century, when the Canadian government started taking concrete steps to amend its colonial policies toward the aboriginal peoples.

Colonization of British Columbia

Long before the European sailors and traders set foot on what later came to be known as North America, the continent was peopled by several native communities belonging to diverse ethnic, linguistic, and cultural groups. Each community had its own social, political, and religious institutions and practices. Fishing and hunting were primary sources of livelihood for these aboriginal communities, which came to be known later as FNs or North American Indians. After Columbus's 'discovery' of America several European navigators explored the continent and established contacts with FN communities. The early English settlements in North America were restricted to New England and the eastern seaboard. For about two hundred years, France and Great Britain fought with each other for control of North America. After the defeat of France in the

H. SRIKANTH

Seven Years' War, the Treaty of Paris was concluded in 1763 wherein France agreed to surrender Quebec, Prince Edward Island, Cape Breton, and New Brunswick to the British. The Royal Proclamation of 1763 set the norms for reorganization of British colonies in the New World.[1] The proclamation expressed the wish to develop friendly relations with the indigenous Indian communities and directed the white settlers to hold back from exploiting and oppressing the natives. It declared that the lands designated by the Crown as Indian territories should not be bought or sold by any private individuals or parties. Only the Crown could acquire Indian lands, that too after negotiating honorable treaties with the FN communities. The British then needed the military and political support of the FNs in their wars against France and later against the emerging American nation. Hence, the treaties that the British colonies concluded with the FNs were then referred to as Peace and Friendship Treaties. As expansion of the fur trade depended on the active involvement and cooperation of the native communities, initially the relations between the British fur trading companies and the Indian communities remained more or less cordial. But this cordiality and reciprocity did not last long. The revolt of 13 American colonies against Great Britain, which came to be viewed as the American Revolution, compelled those loyal to Britain – the United Empire Loyalists – to migrate in thousands to the British colonies in North America. Political compulsion to accommodate the loyalists and also the desire to expand the fur trade forced the British to colonize the territories further west, toward the prairies and the Rocky Mountains.

Even before the British reached the western part of the continent, the territories near the Pacific coast and the islands located nearby had been explored by different European powers. However, it was only in 1778 that the British adventurer James Cook sailed to the Pacific coast and established contact with the Nootka community on Vancouver Island.[2] In 1792, George Vancouver, another British navigator and explorer, reached Burrard Inlet on the Pacific coast. Realizing the hold of the Spanish, Vancouver entered into an agreement with Quadra, the Spanish commander in 1792 for a mutually-beneficial trade partnership.[3] At about this time Alexander Mackenzie, a Euro-Canadian trader associated with the North West Company (NWC) crossed the Rocky Mountains and entered the mainland of what is today called British Columbia. Passing through the territories of a number of FN communities (Sekani, Carrier, Shuswap, and Chilcotin) he reached the villages of Bella Coola in 1793. Although Mackenzie intended to move further toward the Pacific coast he was forced to turn back because of the hostility of Bella Bella, a northern Kwakiutl tribe. A decade later Simon Fraser, another Euro-Canadian trader with a clear eye on fur trade, crossed the Rocky Mountains and passed through the areas inhabited by different Indian tribes, the Carrier, Shuswap, Lillooet, and Thompson River Indians. Delighted with his discovery of high-quality fur-bearing animals in the region, which he named New Caledonia, he built forts at McLeod Lake, Fraser Lake, and Stuart Lake with the intention of establishing bases for fur trade. But before he could reach the Pacific Ocean he encountered the intimidating Musqueam tribal warriors at the mouth of the River Fraser. He retreated immediately with his party and reached the canyon where he was received by a friendly group of Thompson River Indians. In 1807 David Thompson, another trader-explorer of the NWC set off from the Rocky Mountains and established a fort named Kootenae House close to Lake Windermere.[4] While exploring the territories in the Columbia River region, NWC had to compete with the American

H. SRIKANTH

companies. In order to match the American competition, the NWC decided to bury its differences with its rival, the HBC, and united into a powerful monopoly that had control over almost the whole of British North America. With the signing of an agreement in 1821 the new monopoly came into existence with the name and charter of Hudson's Bay Company.

After the takeover of New Caledonia and Columbia, the resurgent HBC received exclusive licence to trade in the area between the Rockies and the Pacific coast.[5] Under the guidance of George Simpson who presided over the HBC's affairs in Canada from 1821 to 1860, the company withstood competition from rival fur traders, sought markets for its fur products in China and established its hold over the FNs engaged in the fur trade. However, almost up to the 1840s the British had to encounter American intrusions into the British colonies in North America. Taking advantage of the absence of a well-defined boundary on the western side between Canada and the US, some aggressive Americans began to justify their right to expand up to Alaska, which they had already taken over from the Russians. As tensions mounted between the British and the Americans it appeared for the moment that there would be another war. However, with each realizing its limitations and the futility of war, the two nations agreed in 1846 to the 49th parallel from the Rockies to the coast as the boundary between the two countries, with Britain retaining the whole of Vancouver Island, although its lower end dropped a little below the line.

With this agreement, the HBC was compelled to give up Columbia Valley. James Douglas who was then acting as Chief Factor at Fort Vancouver in Columbia was instructed to shift to Fort Victoria and operate the company affairs from Vancouver Island. To counter the threat of

American squatter settlements, Vancouver Island was made a Crown Colony in 1849.[6] Taking into consideration his rich experience, Douglas was relieved of company responsibilities and made governor of Vancouver Island in 1851. For some more years the mainland continued to be under the trading licence of the company. But following the discovery of gold along the banks of the Thompson and Fraser rivers several thousand American gold-seekers began to rush to the mainland through Victoria. Appropriate measures to regulate the movements of the gold-seekers became necessary to protect the mainland from possible annexation by the US. As it became clear that the methods used by HBC were no longer adequate to meet the new challenges, the British government made a decision in 1858 to end the company rule and take direct control of the administration of the mainland area and named it British Columbia.[7] James Douglas, who played an important role in regulating the miners and the gold-seekers, was made the governor of the new colony as well. Douglas was in charge of both the colonies from 1858 till his retirement in 1864. After his retirement, Arthur Edward Kennedy was made the governor of Vancouver Island and Frederick Seymour was designated as the governor of BC.

This arrangement did not last long. The recession that hit the colonies during the 1860s compelled them to unite into a single colony. An act of union of Vancouver Island and mainland BC was passed in the British Parliament in November 1866.[8] The united colony took the name of British Columbia, with Victoria as its capital. At about this time, the growing threat from the US and the inability of Great Britain to provide them with military protection compelled the French- and English-speaking colonies of the British in North America, viz., Nova Scotia, New Brunswick, Quebec, and Ontario to think of forming a confederation,[9] leading to the enactment of the British North America (BNA) Act, later known as the Constitution Act, 1867.

Inspired by the birth of the Canadian confederation in their neighborhood, the radicals in the colony of BC, who had been fighting for democratization of BC, began to pressurize its government to negotiate with Ottawa to join the confederation. Compelled by the economic problems and the popular pressures Governor Musgrave held discussions in Ottawa to negotiate the terms of union with Canada. British Columbia agreed to join Canada on condition that a rail link would be built to connect it to the rest of the country within 10 years. The terms of agreement were finally approved and BC became a province of Canada in 1871.[10]

FN Tribes in British Columbia

The territory that came to be known as British Columbia, in short BC, has been the home land for different indigenous communities for thousands of years. Several FN tribal groups inhabit Vancouver Island and mainland BC. The major tribes that inhabit Vancouver Island are the Nootka, Kwakiutl, Cowichan, Nanaimo, Straits Salish, Comox, and the Haida. The coastal areas of mainland BC are populated by the bands belonging to the Tlingit, Tahltan, Gitksan, Tsimshian, Bella Coola, Chilcotin, Coast Salish, Lillooet, and Nisga'a tribes. The Kaska, Slave, Sekani, Beaver, Carrier, Shuswap, Okanagon, and Kootenay tribes are the major interior tribes of BC (See Map 3).[11] The FN tribes of BC can be grouped under five language families: Salishian, Wakashan, Athapaskan, Tlingit, and Haida.[12] The Pacific coastal tribes historically had highly-structured societies with three distinct social strata, viz., the nobles, commoners, and slaves. With the exception of slaves, the members of other social strata occupied a hierarchy of social positions. Traditional villages comprised several graded clans or lineages. Each clan was headed by a chief. The chief of the most powerful and prestigious lineage used to act as the chief of the village. The chiefs and nobles held high-ranking titles and controlled the group-held territories and rights.

Map 3. First Nations of British Columbia

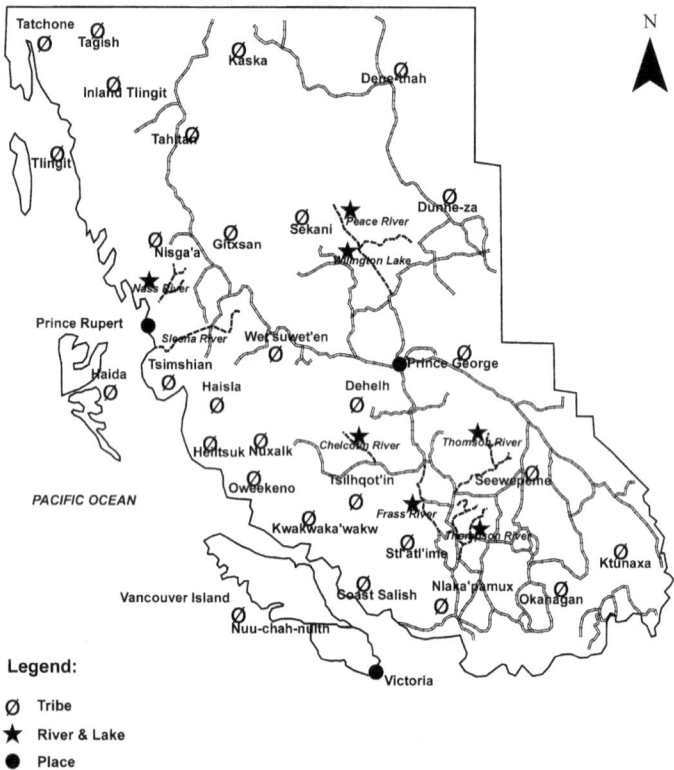

Legend:
Ø   Tribe
★   River & Lake
●   Place

Source: Government of British Columbia, Ministry of Education, Aboriginal Education Enhancement Branch

H. Srikanth

The commoners shared in the group's prestige and provided labor necessary to accumulate food and wealth. The slaves, who made up a considerable part of the native population, were at the bottom of the social hierarchy. They were either purchased or conquered during war. Slaves were treated as chattel and could be sold, given away or even killed. They used to perform all menial and arduous tasks. Their labor was used in productive activities like processing of fish and cutting of timber. Although their physical needs were taken care of by their owners, slaves enjoyed no rights and dignity, being the property of others.[13]

The coastal community relied on the bounty of the sea and the gifts of the forests. They lived on fishing salmon, shellfish, smelts, octopus, crabs, whales, sea lions and sea otters or on hunting. The giant cedar trees gave them raw materials to build canoes, construct longhouses and carve totem poles, weave skirts and make ornaments and other artistic pieces. The coastal tribes which produced surplus engaged in trade with the interior tribes. It is interesting to note that these communities that depended little on agriculture had already developed notions of property and ownership.[14]

Although the land was generally considered as belonging to the village as a whole, they had a sense of personal property. The women owned all the bedding, baskets and other domestic items, while the men owned woodcutting tools, hunting and fishing equipment. Households possessed property in the form of house sites, launching places, places for hunting game, picking berries and gathering roots and bark.[15] Among the coastal tribes ownership included not only material goods but also non-corporeal property such as songs, myths, and knowledge of various types.[16] The coastal tribes had their own customs, religious practices, festivities, and cultural activities. Potlatch, an important ceremony common to all the Pacific coast tribes, was known for its feasting, dancing and gift-giving. During this ceremony, the chiefs would distribute gifts to the invited dignitaries. On such occasions the seating arrangement, order of distribution and value of gifts were carefully planned to reflect the recipients' status. At times potlatches became extravagant and competitive. To outdo their rivals, some chiefs used to give away or destroy enormous quantities of valuable goods in the name of potlatches. Through distribution of wealth in the form of gifts, potlatch used to facilitate public confirmation of an individual's status, inherited rights, and social prestige in the community.[17]

In contrast, the social and ceremonial patterns among the interior tribes in the province were far less complex. They were mostly nomadic and depended on hunting and fishing. The Carrier, Beaver, Sekani, and Slave communities which belong to the Athapaskan language family wandered much of the year in extended families. They had the most rudimentary political organization and no rigid ranking patterns. Compared to them, the Salishian-speaking Thompson River Indians had a more settled pattern of life. They lived in established villages of semi-underground dwellings. During the warm season they went hunting and fishing. Those who resided on the banks of rivers relied mostly on fishing and the others on hunting. They had little or no knowledge of agriculture. Famines were very common in the interior areas. When there was scarcity of fish, moose and deer they survived on small animals like hare.[18] The interior tribes were closely-knit communities living on limited resources. Naturally, they did not need any elaborate and complicated political arrangements. Their societies remained simple and egalitarian compared to their counterparts on the Pacific coast.[19]

H. Srikanth

Inter-village and inter-tribal conflicts were common among both coastal and inland Indians. But full-scale wars over territories were rare. Raiding and warfare were common among the FN tribes. Warfare of the coast people was one of ruse and surprise aimed at obtaining slaves, booty, and the heads of victims. Raids were usually aimed at taking revenge against insults and injuries. After successful raids, the warriors used to burn the houses and turned homeward with their canoes laden with booty, slaves, and the severed heads of their enemies. The Nootkas, who used to wage wars against the Salish and the Kwakiutl, were known head-hunters. They valued the severed heads of their enemies as highly-prized trophies to be hung around the houses as ornaments.[20] The northern people – the Tlingit and the Haida – were known warriors and slave-raiders. At the time of war the warriors wore wooden slat armor, large wooden helmets surmounted with frightening images and carved wooden visors to protect their faces. In times of surplus, the interior tribes also engaged in wars. During warfare, the Okanagans demonstrated great unity against the common enemy.[21]

Fur Trade and FNs in British Columbia

Once the European explorers and traders realized that the soft pelts of sea otters obtained from Vancouver Island had a ready market in China, the vessels of the British, French, Spanish and American traders started vying with one another for pelts along the Pacific coast.[22] The disappearance of fur-bearing animals in east and central Canada also forced the British-Canadian fur traders to cross the Rockies and explore trade avenues in mainland BC. As the fur trade could not be carried out without the support of the FNs who had expertise in hunting such animals, the fur traders entered into trade agreements with the FN communities. Both in Vancouver Island and mainland BC all the native communities were gradually drawn into the fur trade.[23] Initially, the fur traders used to cheat the FNs, taking advantage of their ignorance of the economic significance of the fur trade. But once they realized that the European powers were competing with one another for access to fur supplies, FN communities – including the Indian women – learned the tricks of the trade and became effective bargainers.[24] In exchange for fur, they demanded metal items, firearms and ammunition, blankets, tobacco and alcohol. Initially, the fur trade benefited the traditional communities. The native chiefs of the coast who monopolized or controlled the fur supplies acquired considerable wealth.

The fur trade brought a stimulus to ceremonial life and to the artistic and cultural activities of the coastal people. It also brought about considerable changes in the thinking and lifestyles of the natives.[25] The natives became so obsessed with the white men's goods and tools that they virtually started giving up their own traditional weapons and tools. Availability of guns and ammunition made tribal wars more fierce and deadly. Tribes made every effort to acquire firearms by hook or crook. People started getting addicted to alcohol and at times indulged in criminal acts for a bottle of wine or whisky. The interior tribes began to feel the adverse impact of fur trade in a different way. Once the practice of trapping for sale began to replace hunting for subsistence they became passive dependents on the vicissitudes of the fur economy. As the fur-animal population started dwindling and it became difficult to obtain arms and ammunition from the Europeans the interior tribes found it difficult to return to their bows and arrows.[26]

H. Srikanth

Initially, the FN communities welcomed the European traders and adventurers when they came to this part of North America. More than 30 canoes of the Nootkas warmly received James Cook's ships that sailed into Nootka Sound in 1778. A Nootka chief literally danced and sang in his canoe, greeting the newcomers by waving his bird-shaped rattle. Alexander Mackenzie and Simon Fraser who crossed the Rockies and entered mainland BC also did not encounter any major hostility from the interior tribes. But as fur trade advanced and contacts with European traders became more frequent rifts between the European traders and the natives began to appear. Starting with Captain James Hanna of Macao in 1785, many American sailors-cum-traders looked down upon the FNs and at times overreacted to the acts of defiance and the simple crimes committed by the indigenous people. They insulted the Indian chiefs, used cannons against the native villages, chased and killed the Indians who indulged in stealing or murder. Although the British traders, known respectably as the King George's Men, were not as cruel as their American counterparts, there were occasions when the British also resorted to such inhuman acts in the name of teaching lessons to the native people.

Such punitive measures often resulted in a native backlash. To take revenge against those who insulted and killed them the FNs would attack and plunder the European ships, killing and wounding the officers and crewmen. The British traders responded to the native attacks through cannons and bullets. At times, as punishment, the British stopped trading with the insolent Indian communities and shifted their business to other centers.[27] Since by then the natives had become passively dependent on the fur trade such decisions caused starvation and suffering for them. Although conflicts of such nature continued, the logic of the fur trade demanded some kind of reconciliation and under-standing between the traders and the natives. To the extent their interests were not threatened, the fur traders did not interfere with the native traditions, customs and warfare.[28] Yet, the negative effects of passive dependence by the na-tives on the fur trade became obvious once the fur trade lost its significance by the mid-nineteenth century.

Gold Seekers, Settlers, and Natives

The discovery of coal, first at Beaver Harbor and then at Fort Rupert and later at Nanaimo (all on the east coast of Vancouver Island) gave an opportunity for the HBC to turn from fur trade to mining activities. The Cal-ifornia gold rush stimulated the mining activities in Van-couver Island. The HBC gained a contract to supply coal to the newly-started Pacific Mail Steamership Company which carried mail and miners from Panama to California and the Oregon coast. The growth of mining activities on Vancouver Island and the availability of fertile soil in main-land BC attracted many miners and settlers to the province. Apart from supporting the Puget's Sound Agricultural Company that sought to develop agricultural farms by en-couraging the settlers, HBC itself acquired and sold plots to prospective settlers. Later, the discovery of gold on the banks of the Thompson and Fraser rivers and then in Cari-boo attracted around thirty thousand gold-seekers from the US.[29]

Induced by the gold rush and growth of mining and agricultural activities, thousands of white people came and settled in lands that used to be the hunting and fishing fields of the natives. The increase of non-native settlements cre-ated anxiety in the minds of the natives as they began expe-riencing difficulties in carrying out their traditional

H. SRIKANTH

economic activities. Initially, the natives resisted the entry of the white settlers with all their might.[30] But when thousands started migrating into their territories the natives found it difficult to stop the influx. Unlike the fur traders, who followed the policy of non-interference, the settlers actively engaged in activities that aimed at changing the physical and cultural environment of the region. The miners, gold-seekers, and farmers did not find any need to accommodate the natives.[31]

The economic growth stimulated by those activities did not bring any benefit to the FN communities. Far from it, the loss of the traditional base compelled several native people to migrate to the larger towns and take up the unfamiliar professions of laborers, pimps and prostitutes. The unhygienic conditions in which the migrant natives were forced to live exposed them to several diseases such as measles, tuberculosis, influenza, small pox, and venereal diseases. The natives, who were not immunized against such diseases introduced by the white men, began to die in the thousands. The FN population in BC which was around 70,000 in 1835 was reduced 50 years later to 28,000. The combined population of Nuu-Chah-Nulth and Ditidaht which was estimated to be around 3,500 in 1885 was reduced to 1,605 in 1939.[32] The diseases took such a heavy toll on the natives that their population was reduced by almost three-fourths by the end of the nineteenth century. The premature demise of several chiefs, fishers, hunters, carvers and warriors created a great void in the socio-cultural and political lives of the FN communities. The dwindling native population and the absence of effective leadership considerably weakened the urge and ability of the native communities to resist colonial expansion.

Christian Missionaries and FNs

While the fur traders and settlers deprived the natives of their traditional economic base, the Christian missionaries who entered the province in the name of spreading the gospel among the natives sought to transform the culture and traditions of the Indian communities. They came with the clear goal of 'reforming' and 'civilizing' the FNs and had no qualms about interfering with the traditional customs of the Indians which they considered as barbaric, superstitious and primitive. The indigenous societies appeared to them as dens of darkness and inequity. Many missionaries believed that the native people were dishonest, jealous and lazy. They assumed that the Indians could be saved from degeneration and extinction if they could be turned into red-skinned replicas of Europeans. With the objective of baptizing the natives and turning them toward Christianity, many Christian missionaries came to the province of BC. The Roman Catholics were the first to get in touch with the FN communities of BC. In 1859 Father Charles Pandosy started his missionary work among the Okanogan Indians in mainland BC. William Duncan, deputed by the Anglican Church Missionary Society, started a school at Fort Simpson in 1859. Later, he moved to establish a utopian society at Metlakatla in 1862 where he made several experiments with the Tsimshian Indians with the avowed purpose of 'humanizing and civilizing' them. Later, other missionaries – Roman Catholics, Methodists, Baptists, Presbyterians and others – who worked among different Indian communities followed Duncan's prescriptions.[33]

Governors like Douglas and Seymour also believed that through the spread of Christianity, the natives could be civilized and saved from extinction. Douglas lent support to the Protestant missionaries, though other missionaries were also allowed to work among the Indians. For several years the natives showed little interest in the activities of the missionaries. Yet, in the main they were hospitable to the missionaries and did not create any serious obstacles to missionary work. In the beginning the natives understood little about the gospel and even those who were formally baptized went back to their traditional ways of life. As long as the native societies were strong and vibrant the people found no reason to give up their traditional values and customs. As a result, during the heyday of fur trade the missionaries could not make much headway. However, the loss of control over their land, life and destinies following the colonization of the native territories and the spread of diseases, the Indian communities searching for ways and means to cope with the trauma of the transition period began to respond favorably to the missionary activities.

Christian missionaries played a significant role in initiating several changes in the lives of the Indian communities living in BC. They worked hard to cleanse the natives of superstitious beliefs and obnoxious practices. They discouraged consumption of alcohol and educated the communities about cleanliness and sanitation. During those days when diseases unknown to them played havoc with the lives of the natives, the missionaries provided medical help and mental solace. They taught the natives about European manners, etiquette and habits. Since the missionaries identified 'progress' with European civilization they made efforts to change the ways the native people lived by encouraging them to reside in small residential houses, take to settled agriculture, and work hard to improve their living conditions. There were times when the missionaries openly confronted the colonial authorities and white settlers and lent support to the native claims for more land so that they could turn to agriculture and become economically self-sufficient. The knowledge of English imparted by missionary schools played a very important role in bringing a sense of unity and understanding among the FN tribes.

While recognizing the good work done by the missionaries, one should not, however, ignore the adverse impact that their activities also had on the natives' lives. Their belief in the supremacy of Christianity and European traditions made them take extreme stands against everything native. They hated and opposed animistic practices, shamanism and ancestral worship. Some missionaries openly advocated an official ban on potlatch and other traditional native ceremonies. They taught the natives to leave the longhouses and stay in small, single-family, European houses.[34] More than all these things, the manner in which the missionaries ran residential schools came up for sharp criticism. The Canadian government made rules such as mandatory attendance and provided necessary funding to the missionaries for running the schools.

The missionaries, with the declared objective of 'civilizing the savages' forcibly took native children away from their traditional environment and educated them in residential schools in Christian and Euro-Canadian ways. By giving the children new names, preventing them from speaking their mother tongues, imposing strict discipline and severe punishments for non-compliance or defiance, the missionary-run residential schools attempted to wean the native children away from their culture, language, and traditions. There were allegations of physical, psychological, and even sexual abuse of children in these schools. The missionary schools in a way contributed to the disappearance of native languages and the loss of traditional knowledge about healing, parenting, and social relations. Extended periods of schooling led to the breakdown of fam-

H. Srikanth

ilies. Children returning from the schools were often found unable to communicate with their parents and had little in common with them.[35] Far from making them strong and self-confident, missionary schools promoted a complex of inferiority among the young persons and made them deviants. The trauma that the native children underwent was so much that the natives today have forgotten much of the good work done by the Christian missionaries and only remember all that went wrong with the residential schools.[36]

The Natives as Wards of the Crown

The colonial authorities could not remain mute spectators to the growing differences between the natives and non-natives. The compulsions of colonial expansion required more and more migrants from outside to come and settle in the colonies and expand agricultural and industrial activities. But large-scale influx of settlers would generate fear and insecurity among the FN communities. Unplanned colonial expansion would generate more tensions and lead to riotous outbursts. Hence, it was essential for the colonial authorities to minimize the chances of direct confrontation between the FNs and the white settlers by ensuring security to the native population and support to the white settlers. James Douglas, who was appointed as the first governor of the colony of Vancouver Island (1851–58) and later became governor of the whole of BC (1858–64), very effectively carried out this balancing act.

During the first four years of his tenure as governor of Vancouver Island he negotiated 14 agreements, which later came to be known as the "Douglas Treaties," with the FN communities and acquired land measuring around 358 sq m in and around Victoria, Nanaimo, and Fort Rupert. In return for surrendering their land the natives were confirmed in possession of their village sites and fields for their and their future generations' use. The natives were assured of their right to hunt and fish over and in the unoccupied lands.[37] In most cases the purchases were not made in cash but in the form of blankets whose value was inflated several times. The entire Victoria area, for example, was obtained for just 371 blankets.[38]

By purchasing land through treaties Douglas sought to ensure unencumbered land for the expansion of white settlements. He sought to negotiate similar treaties with other Indian communities also. But due to the paucity of funds he could not go ahead with any new agreements after 1854. However, after he took charge as governor of BC, instead of negotiating treaties, Douglas created reserves with the avowed purpose of protecting the FN communities from encroachment by white settlers. The reserves included the village locations, burial sites, and land for agricultural and fishing purposes. He wanted the Indian communities to treat the reserves as their own inheritance. The reserves were deemed to be the collective property of the whole community. As such no Indian had any authority to sell or alienate the reserve land to any private individuals or parties. For determining the size of the reserves, he instructed his officers to ensure that all families living in the village got a minimum of 10 acres each. Although in comparison to Canadian standards prescribed in Ontario and the Prairies the reserves created by Douglas were very small in size, there was a compensating element there. Instead of confining the Indians to reserves, Douglas wanted the Indians to add to their possessions and devote their earnings to the purchase of property outside their reserves. He expected the FNs to be treated as British subjects endowed with full civil and political rights, including the right to vote and to preempt vacant Crown land.[39] This foresighted liberal pol-

H. SRIKANTH

icy of Douglas' aimed at reconciling the conflicting interests of the natives and the non-natives was, however, given up once he stepped down as governor of Vancouver Island and BC in 1864. The persons who succeeded him as governor did not have the same altruistic and ideological bent of mind. As they were more preoccupied with political and economic issues concerning the integration of the two colonies, the Indian policy was virtually left to Joseph Trutch, Chief Commissioner of Lands and Works.

Unlike Douglas, Trutch had no respect or concern for the FNs. He viewed them as hindrances to the progress of civilization. He looked down upon the Indians as uncivilized savages, basically ugly and lazy, and lawless and violent.[40] By maintaining that the Indian communities had no society, government, and laws and that the reserves were only generous gifts from the Crown, Trutch contributed to the rise of white racist ideology in BC. The Colonial Land Ordinance of 1870 reversed the policies of Douglas. It denied the natives of the right to preempt land and forced the Indians to confine themselves to the reserves.[41] Taking advantage of the dwindling population of the Indians, the size of many reserves in BC were considerably reduced by setting 10 acres per family as the maximum limit. It was unfortunate that Trutch, who initiated such anti-Indian policies and programs, happened to represent the united colony of BC in its negotiations with Ottawa for joining the Canadian confederation. As a member of the delegation he misled the dominion leaders about the actual status of the Indian communities in BC and made them believe that the colony was following a liberal and generous policy toward the natives. The authorities in Ottawa took the claims of officials like Trutch at face value and made no effort to verify the authenticity of the claims made.[42]

With BC agreeing to join the confederation the charge of the Indians and the trusteeship and management of the lands reserved for their use and benefit became the responsibility of the dominion government. Ottawa maintained that while creating the reserves the government should ensure at least 80 acres per family of five. To make way for smooth colonization, by 1871 the dominion government had negotiated 11 treaties with the FNs across the country. Almost all the federal treaties provided for reserve lands, monetary payments, medical help, ammunition, and suits every three years to chiefs and headmen. When the Canadian authorities came to know about the plight of the FNs in BC they tried to pressurize the province to enlarge the reserves, but provincial politicians refused to adopt the land-surrender treaty model pursued in other parts of Canada, arguing that they had unilaterally extinguished the aboriginal titles.[43]

The attempts of officials like Gilbert Sproat, then Indian reserve commissioner to re-establish some of the land policies of Douglas failed to yield results as the authorities in Ottawa did not dare to antagonize the political leaders in BC.[44] Since assignment of land was a provincial responsibility as per the terms of union of 1871 the dominion government could do little on the issue of allocation of land to the natives. In 1875 George Walkem, then premier of BC, maintained that small reserves had the promising advantage of forcing native people into wage work in the larger society.[45] Yet, due to the persistent demands and protests of the Beaver, Slave, and Sekani Indians of northeastern BC, in 1899 the federal government extended Treaty 8 to some parts of BC. Despite its qualms the provincial government chose not to object to the treaty as it had no obligation to pay money or provide land for the reserves. Except for the areas covered under Treaty 8, the rest of BC continued to be

H. Srikanth

a province with hundreds of reserves, but many without valid federal or provincial treaties.

Differences in their approaches should not let one ignore the commonalities between the dominion and provincial authorities. With the loss of commercial and military relevance, the Canadian government also began seeing the Indians as impediments to colonial expansion. Cooperation soon gave way to coercion. The Indians were removed from the land by concluding treaties and creating reserves. They were subjected to an intensive program of assimilation through residential schools, evangelization, and legislation.[46] The Canadian government passed the Indian Act of 1876 to exercise control over the lives of the FNs.[47] The Act classified the Indians as status and non-status Indians and made arbitrary rules as to who should or should not be considered as Indians. In the reserve areas, replacing the rule by traditional chiefs, the Indian Act instituted uniform band governments with elected chiefs. The elected band councils were given few powers of decision making and they had to be dependent on the Department of Indian Affairs for all financial and administrative support. Unlike municipal corporations, the native band councils did not have clear legal status.[48] The agents appointed by the department were given enormous powers to monitor and regulate the bands and their governments.[49] In 1920 there were 16 Indian agents in the province responsible for the protection of native rights and for instructing the native people about civilized ways. The Indian Act was amended from time to time to assign more and more powers of control to the officials over the Indians and their reserve lands.

In the name of civilizing the tribes the educated Indians were enfranchised and deregistered as Indians. In 1885 the Department of Indian Affairs instituted a pass system prohibiting outsiders from doing business with FNs without permission from the Indian agent. In 1916 the federal and provincial governments passed legislation removing extensive tracts of valuable land from many reserves in the province. In 1924 the federal government passed a bill legally enabling the government to reduce the size of the reserves without the consent of the natives.[50] All these Acts and actions of the federal government which had a vital bearing on the lives of the Indian communities in all Canadian provinces, including those inhabiting BC, make it clear that there were no qualitative differences between the dominion and provincial governments as far as the interests of Indians were concerned. As the FNs started organizing themselves to protect their aboriginal rights both governments joined together to suppress the Indian activism. Measures such as banning of potlatch in 1884, amendment of the Indian Act in 1927 in prohibiting collection of funds for pro-land claim activities, and the 1943 agreement between BC and Canada supporting provincial jurisdiction over mineral resources in the reserves[51] show the identity of interests between the two.

Native Activism against Colonial Domination

During the heyday of fur trade the FN communities insisted that the foreign traders treat them as equals in partnership. Whenever any Indian community felt that its people were cheated or humiliated by the white traders it revolted against them instantly. On several occasions the FN communities took up arms against the colonial domination. As long as the natives were in a majority they felt secure and confident. But as the settler population started growing conflicts between the natives and non-natives became more frequent. It was basically to ward off violent confrontations that Douglas planned to create reserves and

H. SRIKANTH

guarantee natives their aboriginal rights for fishing and hunting even in the areas ceded by them. However, the reserves, which were supposed to protect the natives against the white settlers, in course of time turned into a sort of ghettos system. Unlike as in other provinces the reserves in BC were small, congested, and insufficient for agricultural activities. At the time of its entry into the Canadian federation there were 120 reserves in BC. Although the Indians in BC accounted for 17 percent of the total Indian population in Canada the total reserve area in the province was only 344,000 hectares or 13 percent of the whole of Canada.[52]

Unlike as in other provinces where reserves were created as part of treaties most reserves in BC were created through executive decision, not through legally valid treaties. The natives as such could not claim any legal rights over the reserve lands, as they could be taken away at any time by the colonial authorities for the benefit of the white settlers. The native rights to preempt Crown land and to hunt and fish beyond the reserve boundaries were curtailed. Outside the reserve all provincial land was opened to capital and settlers and consequently for all practical purposes the aboriginal rights of usage, customs, and native law got extinguished. All this gave birth to a regime of private property that aimed at detaching ownership of land from use rights and making it accessible and responsive to the market.[53]

Certain indigenous communities made attempts to adjust to the needs of the white economy and tried to enter agriculture, commercial fishing, logging, mining, and industry. However, the natives could not break out of the periphery, as they did not have enough resources and administrative support.[54] In the field of politics they were totally marginalized. Many vital political decisions like fixing the boundary line between Canada and the US, the union of the colonies of Vancouver Island and BC, the decision of BC to join the Canadian confederation, and others were taken without consulting the FNs. The Indian Act and residential schools were used to 'discipline' the natives and keep them under constant surveillance. The diseases spread by the white settlers in the second half of the nineteenth century killed thousands of natives and nearly wiped off several native communities in BC. With the demise of leaders and the disruption of social organizations the native communities in BC became politically and militarily so weak that they found themselves powerless to resist the growing onslaught of colonialism. Taking advantage of their weakness, the colonial authorities further subjugated the Indian population, making them wards in their own land and denying them rights over their own territories and destinies.

Resurgence of FN Movement

The tribal groups inhabiting the province of BC had little in common. They did not have a common culture, language, or political tradition. Yet, the history of common subjection of all Indian tribes to colonial domination gave birth to a pan-Indian consciousness among the native tribes. However, unlike the US where a pan-Indian consciousness developed above specific tribal identities, the pan-Indianism in BC developed alongside the growth of tribal identities. Although the development of the English language as a lingua franca, expansion of the transport network, and the experiment of residential schools did strengthen pan-Indian consciousness to some extent, all these could not succeed in imparting liberal individualistic consciousness among the FNs. Individualistic pan-Indianism of the US type did not develop in Canadian provinces as the reserves were created in their own respective traditional village sites and most tribes were settled on their traditional land and were not sufficiently exposed to the influence of the families and ideas of the white people. In such circumstances it was natural that native activism could not detach itself from tribal consciousness.[55]

The persistence of tribal identities should not, however, lead one to conclude that the Indian communities failed to change in tune with the changing circumstances. They were pragmatic enough to realize that they could not revert to the pre-colonial period. They understood that in the changed conditions it was not possible for the FN communities to take to violent means to overthrow the colonial yoke. Most of them did realize the fact that they had to live with the white settlers who had established themselves in the province and made it their homeland. Hence, on several occasions the natives expressed their willingness to share their land and resources with the white settlers. But at the same time they demanded that Canada recognize their inherent aboriginal rights and treat them fairly as equal partners, not as wards. Taking advantage of the liberal democratic institutions of Canada they worked hard to create a space for themselves within the colonial framework. Through letters, petitions, demonstrations, public debates and protest meetings, the Indian communities tried to make aboriginal rights a political issue. They effectively argued that their land had been taken away and that their aboriginal rights were extinguished unilaterally without their consent. They demanded larger reserves, treaties, and self-government under British law.[56] It was because of the persistent efforts of some of the interior tribes that territories measuring one hundred thousand square miles were covered under Treaty 8.

In 1906 three Indian chiefs of the province petitioned the king of England directly. By influencing citizens' groups the native activists brought pressure on the government to refer the issue of aboriginal titles in BC to the higher courts. In 1913, arguing that they had neither ceded their land to anyone nor had been defeated in war by anyone, the Nisga'a laid claim to Nass Valley and petitioned Ottawa for redress.[57] In 1915 the Allied Indian Tribes of British Columbia, the first province wise native political activist group came into existence. Apart from lobbying politicians in Victoria and Ottawa the organization threatened to move the highest court of the UK for seeking legal remedy. To prevent the FNs from going to the courts and to stop their political activities the federal government amended the Indian Act in 1927 making it illegal and hence punishable for any attempt at raising funds for pursuing the land claims. The move temporarily put a halt to native activism for the next two decades.

However, the situation of Indians started changing for the better after the Second World War. During the war thousands of FN citizens joined the Canadian forces to fight the Nazis. This initiative helped in changing the government's perceptions about them. Recognizing their services and sacrifices during the war BC decided to grant franchise to all registered Indians in 1947.[58] Although Parliament abolished judicial appeals to England, in 1951 the federal government revoked the ban on land claims that had been in effect since 1927. The government also amended the Indian Act in 1951 to retract the ban on potlatch. With liberal governments assuming power, the postwar world threw open new opportunities for reconciliation between the FNs and the Canadian government.

Notes and References

1. "The Royal Proclamation of October 7, 1763," Virtual Law Office, http://www.bloorstreet.com/200block/rp1763.htm accessed 7 July 2008.

2. Robin Fisher, *Contact and Conflicts: Indian–European Relations in British Columbia, 1774–1890* (Vancouver: UBC Press, 1992), 2.

3. George Woodcock, *British Columbia: A History of the Province* (Vancouver and Toronto: Douglas & McIntyre, 1994), 28–30.

4. Ibid., 39–49.

5. Ibid., 48.

6. Barry M. Gough, "The Character of the British Columbia Frontier", *BC Studies* 32 (Winter 1976–77): 28–40.

7. Gerald Walsh, *Indians in Transition: An Inquiry Approach* (Toronto: McClelland and Stewart, 1971), 84.

8. Woodcock, *British Columbia*, 113–20.

9. Rand Dyck, *Canadian Politics: Critical Perspectives*, 26; D. G. Creighton, "The United States and Canadian Confederation," in *Readings in Canadian History: Pre-Confederation*, ed. Douglas Francis and Donald B. Smith (Toronto: Holt, Rinehart and Winston of Canada, 1986), 461–71; *Canada: One Hundred Years 1867–1967* (Ottawa: Dominion Bureau of Statistics, 1967), 15–19.

10. Woodcock, *British Columbia*, 121–4.

11. Robert J. Muckle, *The First Nations of British Columbia: An Anthropological Survey* (Vancouver: UBC Press, 1998), 117–22.

12. McMillan and Yellowhorn, *First Peoples in Canada* (Vancouver: Douglas McIntyre, 2004), 5–8, 191.

13.Ibid., 208.

14. Paul Tennant, *Aboriginal Peoples and Politics: The Indian Land Question in British Columbia 1849–1989* (Vancouver: UBC Press, 1990), 6–7.

15. *Our Native People – Nootka*, Series 1, Vol. 5 (Victoria: British Columbia Heritage Series, 1996).

16. Tom Flanagan, *First Nations?: Second Thoughts* (Toronto: McGill-Queen's University Press), 117.

17. Mcmillan and Yellowhorn, *First Peoples*, 209: Woodcock, *British Columbia*, 16–18.
18. Woodcock, *British Columbia*, 21.
19. Tennant, *Aboriginal Peoples*, 8.
20. *Our Native Peoples – Nootka*, 47.
21. Peter Carstens, *The Queen's People, A Study of Hegemony, Coercion and Accommodation among the Okanagan of Canada* (Toronto: University of Toronto Press, 1991), 9–24.
22. Alan D. Mcmillan, *Since the Time of the Transformers: The Ancient Heritage of the Nuu-Chah-Nulth, Ditidaht, and Makah* (Vancouver: UBC Press, 1999), 179.
23. Fisher, *Contact and Conflicts*, 1–23.
24. Woodcock, *British Columbia*; Sylvia Van Kirk, "'Women in Between': Indian Women in Fur Trade Society," in Francis and Smith, *Readings in Canadian History*, 174–89.
25. Arthur J. Ray, "Introduction: Native People in British Columbia," *Native Studies Review*, 11:1 (1996): 167–70.
26. Woodcock, *British Columbia*, 54.
27. Fisher, *Contact and Conflicts*, 35–9.
28. Ibid., 47.
29. Woodcock, *British Columbia*, 93.
30. Fisher, *Contact and Conflicts*, 70.
31. Ibid., 96–8.
32. L. F. S. Upton, "Contact and Conflict on the Atlantic and Pacific Coasts of Canada," *Acadiensis* 9:2 (1980): 3–13; also Alan D. Mcmillan, *Since the Time of the Transformers: The Ancient Heritage of the Nuu-Chah-Nulth, Ditidaht, and Makah* (Vancouver, UBC Press, 1999), 191–5.
33. Fisher, *Contact and Conflicts*, 131–6.
34. Susan M. Kenyon, *The Kyuquot Way: A Study of a West Coast (Nootkan) Community* (Ottawa: National Museums of Canada, 1980), 54–61.
35. Muckle, *First Nations*, 65–7; Noel Dyck, *What is the Indian 'Problem': Tutelage and Resistance in Canadian Indian Administration* (Newfoundland: Institute of Social and Economic Research, 1991), 81–3.
36. Muckle, *First Nations*, 68–9.
37. Tennant, *Aboriginal Peoples*, 19–20.
38. McMillan and Yellowhorn, *First Peoples*, 320.
39. Tennant, *Aboriginal Peoples*, 26–35.

40. John Borrows, "Re-Living the Present: Title, Treaties and Trickster in British Columbia," *BC Studies: The British Columbia Quarterly*, 120 (Winter 1998-9), 101.
41. Chief Joe Mathias and Gary R. Yabsley, "Conspiracy of Legislation: The Suppression of Indian Rights in Canada," *BC Studies*, 89 (Spring 1991): 35.
42. Tennant, *Aboriginal Peoples*, 44-5.
43. Gerald Walsh, *Indians in Transition: An Inquiry Approach* (Toronto: McClelland and Stewart, 1971), 96; Flanagan, *First Nations?*, 124-5.
44. Fisher, *Contact and Conflicts*, 186-99.
45. Cole Harris, *Making Native Space: Colonialism, Resistance, and Reserves in British Columbia* (Vancouver: UBC Press, 2002), 283.
46. J. R. Miller, *Skyscrapers Hide the Heavens: A History of Indian-White Relations in Canada* (Toronto: University of Toronto Press, 1989).
47. James S. Frideres, *Native People in Canada: Contemporary Conflicts* (Ontario: Prentice-Hall Canada, 1983), 20-32.
48. John L. Tobias, "Protection, Civilization, Assimilation: An Outline History of Canada's Indian Policy," in Ian Getty and Antoina Lussier, *As Long as the Sun Shines and the Water Flows* (Vancouver: UBC Press, 1983), 39-53; Jill Wherret, *Aboriginal Self-government* (Ottawa: Library of Parliament, 1996), 3.
49. Harris, *Making Native Space*, 268-74.
50. Mathias and Yabsley, "Conspiracy of Legislation", 35; Muckle, *First Nations*, 71.
51. Muckle, *First Nations*, 72-3.
52. Melvin H. Smith, *Our Home or Native Land?: What Government's Aboriginal Policy is Doing to Canada* (Victoria: Crown Western, 1995), 78.
53. Harris, *Making Native Space*, 266.
54. Ray, "Native People," 1-3.
55. Tennant, *Aboriginal Peoples*, 68-74.
56. Ibid., 50.
57. Smith, *Our Home*, 81.
58. Tennant, *Aboriginal Peoples*, 49.

H. Srikanth

3

BRITISH COLONIALISM AND HILL
TRIBES OF COMPOSITE ASSAM

In view of the variations in colonial experiences, the nature and forms of struggles of indigenous peoples also differ from country to country. The previous chapter discussed the experiences and struggles of the Native Indians in the Canadian province of British Columbia (BC) during the colonial phase. In a way the Native Indian experience in BC throws light on the manner in which European colonialism operated and affected the indigenous peoples in the Americas and Oceania. Tens of thousands of white immigrants who came and settled in these sparsely-populated territories virtually overpowered the native peoples and took control of their lands and other resources. In course of time the white settlers severed their relations with their parent countries in Europe and built their own states in the colonies. These states claimed allegiance to liberal democratic ideas and ideals. They gave shape to constitutional governments and developed representative institutions. But when it came to the aboriginal peoples the governments continued to treat them as second-grade citizens and denied them equal rights. Although the leaders of these nations took the position that colonialism had formally come to an end long back, their policies toward the indigenous peoples continued to be colonial and racist in content till the mid-twentieth century. But this history of indigenous peoples in advanced capitalist countries like Canada, the US, Australia and New Zealand was not replicated in the colonies and semi-colonies of Asia and Africa. The colonial history of India makes this difference clear.

British Colonialism in the Indian Subcontinent

Unlike the Americas and Oceania the densely-populated Indian subcontinent has a well-recorded civilizational history dating back thousands of years. When the British East India Company came to India in 1600 in search of trade opportunities, mainland India, then under the rule of the Mughal emperors, had already achieved high levels of social and economic development.[1] By then the subcontinent had a highly stratified society and the elite occupying higher positions in society and polity had access to as many comforts and amenities as their counterparts in the European states used to enjoy during that period. Yet the elite constituted only a minority of the population. The majority of the people were peasants and artisans living mostly in the villages. Irrespective of whether the ruler was a Hindu, Muslim or Sikh, the people living in organized villages were regulated by the caste system. However, apart from these highly stratified social groups of people who identified themselves as belonging to particular castes, some pockets in the subcontinent were inhabited by tribal communities, which were less stratified, non-acquisitive, endogamous units living outside the caste system. They lived mostly in the forests and hill areas and depended mostly on shifting cultivation, hunting and food-gathering for their livelihood. The tribals had their own distinct dialects, cultures, traditions, and sociopolitical organizations. Although some tribes were led by powerful chiefs who were often considered by others as tribal kings, they lacked organized state systems with all the paraphernalia. Indian history and

H. SRIKANTH

mythology mention several conflicts and confrontations between the tribal and non-tribal communities in India. Despite the contradictions between the two, the dominant mainstream non-tribal communities in the subcontinent did recognize the aboriginal rights of the tribal communities and allowed them considerable autonomy to live in accordance with their traditions and customs.

Initially when the East India Company came to India the British had to deal with different kings and emperors. By successfully playing one native ruler against another and by outplaying the other European competitors the East India Company acquired political control over different territories in mainland India.[2] Apart from annexing the territories under the control of feudal kings and emperors, the British took over the areas inhabited and controlled by the tribal communities. Paying scant respect to the aboriginal rights of the tribal communities, the British took control of the forests, brought lands held by tribal communities under the zamindari system, and imposed bureaucratic restrictions on the tribals' access to their traditional land and forests. Introduction of colonial regimes of control, imposition of taxes, development of property relations, expansion of market, and restrictions imposed on shifting cultivation worsened the plight of tribal communities. Having lost their political autonomy and control over sources of livelihood, several tribal communities in mainland India were marginalized. The colonial authorities did little to alleviate the sufferings of the tribal communities in mainland India.[3] Interestingly, the British had to adopt a slightly different kind of policy with regard to the indigenous communities, as they began to expand toward the northeast frontier of India.

By the end of the eighteenth century the British had established their control over the whole of Bengal up to Golpara and Mymensingh in the east. The territory beyond this part of Bengal comprised several valleys and hill ranges which were still under the control of different native rulers and tribal chiefs. Map 4 shows hill and valley areas of India's northeastern region. The native people of the region were racially very different from the people of mainland India. Although the traditional life of the natives in some parts of the region was influenced by the dominant religious and cultural traditions prevalent in mainland India, the native kingdoms and communities in the region never came under the political control of the empires that had ruled India up until then. For a long time, the British also did not evince any interest in extending their control beyond Bengal. As they were then keen on consolidating their authority over mainland India, initially even the British colonizers followed the policy of non-interference with regard to this region, which they named the North-East Frontier of Bengal.[4] Despite the fact that the company did intervene on behalf of the Ahom ruler of Brahmaputra Valley at the time of the Moamaria revolt and later entered into a commercial treaty with the Ahom king in 1793, the British were still not keen on extending their control over the region.

Hill Tribes of the North-East Frontier of Bengal

At the time of the British contact the Brahmaputra Valley, inhabited by different communities like the Bodos, Koches, Chutias, Moamarias, etc. was under the Ahom rule. The hills surrounding the Brahmaputra Valley and also those adjoining the Surma Valley in Bengal were inhabited by several indigenous hill communities.[5] The

H. Srikanth

Bhutias, Akas, Duflas, Hill Miris, and Abors inhabited the foothills of the Himalayas north of River Brahmaputra. The hills located on the northeastern side of the Brahmaputra river surrounding Sadiya were occupied by the Khamtis, Mishmis, and Singphos. On the eastern side bordering Burma (now Myanmar) are the Naga Hills peopled by different Naga tribes. On the west of the Naga Hills are the Mikir Hills (Karbi-Anglong) and North Cachar Hills populated by the Karbis, Dimasas, Hmars and other hill communities. The southern hill ranges adjoining the Naga Hills are occupied by the Tangkhul Nagas and the Kukis. The hills south of Golpara and north of Surma Valley are inhabited by the Garos, Khasis, and Jaintias. South of the Cachar plains are the Hill Tipperah and Lushai Hills where communities like the Tripuris, Lushais, Pawis, Lakhers, and others lived. Map 5 gives an idea of distribution of tribes in composite Assam in 1842.

In view of certain common attributes like lack of marked internal class differentiation, absence of advanced notions of private property, dominance of animistic practices, and endogamous relations, the British termed the hill communities of Assam "tribes." Racially, the hill communities were referred to as mongoloid, but culturally and linguistically they belonged to different groups. Each tribe had its own dialect, culture, political institutions, and religious practices.[6] While most of them were indeed animists, some like the Jaintias and Dimasas were Hinduized and tribes like the Bhutias, Monpas, and Khamtis followed Buddhism.[7] Barring the Garos, Jaintias, and Khasis which were matrilineal communities, all other hill tribes were patrilinial and patriarchal.

Map 4. North-East India showing Hill and Plain Areas of Composite Assam

N

CHINA

TIBET

Arunachal Pradesh

BHUTAN

Assam

Karbi Anglong Hills

Nagaland

Meghalaya

North Cachar Hills

BANGLADESH

Manipur

MYANMAR

Tripura

Mizoram

Legend:

------- Borders of Composite Assam
Hill Areas of Composite Assam
Former Princely States Outside Assam
Assam Plain Areas

Scale:

1   0.5   0   1 Kilometers

H. SRIKANTH

Map 5. Distribution of Tribes in Assam in 1842

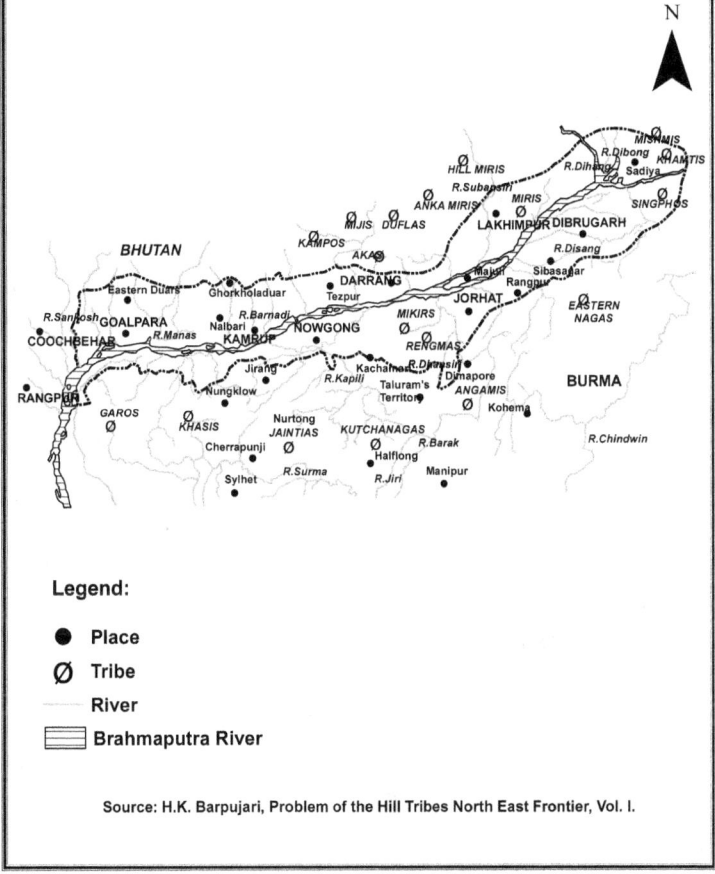

N

MISHMIS
HILL MIRIS   R.Dibong   KHAMTIS
R.Dihong   Sadiya
R.Subansiri
ANKA MIRIS   MIRIS   SINGPHOS
MIJIS   DUFLAS   LAKHIMPUR DIBRUGARH

BHUTAN   KAMPOS
AKAS   R.Disang
Maibi   Sibasagar
Eastern Duars   Ghorkholaduar   DARRANG   Rangpur
Tezpur   JORHAT   EASTERN
R.Santosh GOALPARA   R.Barnadi   MIKIRS   NAGAS
Nalbari   NOWGONG
COOCHBEHAR   R.Manas   KAMRUP   RENGMAS
Jirang   Kachaman R.Dhansiri
R.Kapili   Tairam's   Dimapore   BURMA
RANGPUR   Nungklow   Territory   ANGAMIS
Kohema
GAROS   Nurtong   R.Chindwin
KHASIS   JAINTIAS   KUTCHANAGAS
Cherrapunji   R.Barak
Halflong
Sylhet   R.Surma   R.Jiri   Manipur

Legend:

● Place
Ø Tribe
— River
▤ Brahmaputra River

Source: H.K. Barpujari, Problem of the Hill Tribes North East Frontier, Vol. I.

Almost all tribal communities had migrated to the present region of their habitation from the East or Southeast Asian countries at some time in history. Politically, these communities were at different stages of development. One could see state formation among certain hill communities such as the Jaintias and Dimasas.[8] Some tribes like Akas, Khamptis, and Singphos had powerful chieftainships and used to exercise control over the weaker tribes. The Lushai chiefs were oppressive and despotic. The Naga chiefs were comparatively more democratic.[9] The Khasis had their own semi-oligarchic political institutions known as *himas*. For lack of an appropriate equivalent term in English, the *himas* were referred to as Khasi States, although they did not have organized armies, a bureaucracy and prisons. The *himas* were headed by *syiems* who were selected from among certain privileged clans among the Khasis. The powers of the *syiems* were not absolute and an aristocracy of a native type controlling and monitoring the *syiems* existed.[10]

Despite the fact that the tribes relied on hunting, fishing and food-gathering for their livelihood almost all the hill communities had some knowledge of agriculture as well. While most communities practiced shifting cultivation a few such as the Aos and Angamis had knowledge of wet cultivation as well.[11] They ate fish and meat and their staple food was rice. Since what was produced in the hills was not sufficient to meet all their material requirements the hill tribes had to find outlets in the plains for trade and for cultivable lands. The hill tribes came down to *hats*, village markets situated near *duars* (mountain passages) to sell their forest and mineral products and exchange required goods from the cultivators and traders from the plains. Such trading and business activities were necessary for the hill communities and were very profitable for the traders in the plains.[12]

The hill people were often cheated and exploited by the traders and landlords of the plains. As retaliation, they used to plunder the villages and take away men and materials from the plains. Some tribes such as the Mizos and

Khamptis used to engage persons kidnapped from the plains as slaves and use their services in agriculture and other productive activities.[13] The slave trade was rampant among certain hill tribes. Unless ransomed, they sold the kidnapped persons to merchants in neighboring districts. To prevent tribal attacks the Ahom rulers used to allocate some cultivable lands in the plains to tribes inhabiting the hill areas adjoining the Ahom kingdom. The people in some plain areas were paying *posa*, a kind of ransom or blackmail, every year in the form of food, materials, cloth, ornaments, slaves and other requirements to the hill tribes. Whereas the hill tribes considered *posa* their right, the people in the plains looked upon it as an inescapable obligation. There were disputes between the hill tribes and the people in the plains over the issue of *posa*.[14]

Apart from such friction between the hill tribes and the people from the plains there were also inter-tribal, intra-tribal and inter-village conflicts among the hill communities. Memories of old animosities, competition for control of resources, fear of outsiders, and their wish to protect the community interests at any cost engendered several bloody conflicts. In the villages the men would brawl and quarrel for revenge or pride. Head-hunting and human sacrifice were prevalent among the Garos, Nagas, and Lushais. Like the Nootka of BC,[15] the wild tribes of northeast India also took pride in collecting and exhibiting the severed heads of their enemies. Tribal conflicts used to cause considerable bloodshed, destruction and forced displacement of communities.

British Colonial Expansion in India's Northeast

Initially, the British had no knowledge of the different hill communities inhabiting the region. It was only in the second decade of the nineteenth century that the company sent David Scott, magistrate of Rangpur, to investigate the causes for tribal revolts against the zamindars (landlords) of Golpara that the British came in touch with the Garos living in the hills bordering Golpara and Mymensingh. At about this time, taking advantage of the political uncertainties and anarchy prevailing in the region, the Burmese ruler invaded the Ahom kingdom and also took control of the Manipuri and Cachari kingdoms. The Burmese governor warned the British against intervention on behalf of the Ahoms. Realizing the vulnerability of the eastern frontier of Bengal, the British gave up their policy of non-interference and decided to take on the Burmese troops. In the war that they decided to wage, the British needed the support of all native kings and tribal chiefs in the region. David Scott, who by then had become the agent to the governor-general for the North-East Frontier of Bengal, gave a public proclamation to all the inhabitants of the region requesting them to join their fight against the Burmese invaders.[16]

The proclamation stated that the British were not led into Assam by the thirst of conquest, but were forced into the war for self-defense. The company assured that after defeating the common foe it would reestablish a government suited to the wants and interests of the native people. In 1824 Scott entered into treaties with the king of Jaintia and the Khasi chief of Nongkhlaw. The company sought men and material support from the native communities and also right of passage for British troops through their territories.[17] With the support of the native communities the British forces drove away the Burmese troops and forced the Burmese chief to surrender at Rangpur in 1825. Realizing that the Burmese invasion could become possible only because of the help rendered by some of the hill tribes, especially the Singphos, the British troops moved beyond Sadiya into Singpho territory and drove the Burmese and their allies out of the Singpho villages. Similarly, the British troops were sent from Sylhet to liberate Manipur and Cachar. Fearing defeat at the hands of the British forces the Burmese troops withdrew from both the kingdoms, paving the way for the British to reinstate Gambir Singh and Gobind Chandra as rulers of Manipur and Cachar, respectively. Finally, the British forced the king of Ava to sign the Yandaboo Treaty in 1826 whereby the Burmese king gave up all his claims over the Ahom, Manipuri, and Cachari kingdoms. British officers also made treaties with the chiefs of the Moamarias, Khamptis, and Singphos in 1826 to ensure that they would not side with the Burmese but help the British in their war efforts against possible invasions by the Burmese.[18]

Contact with Hill Tribes of Northeast India

Once the immediate threat of Burmese invasion disappeared the British made efforts to bring some kind of administrative and political order in the Ahom territory, affected by palace intrigues and tribal revolts. Having by then emerged as de facto rulers in the valley, the British were no longer willing to withdraw from the region. Apart from their strategic considerations to protect the frontiers of Bengal, the British, who by then had become aware of the economic potentialities of the region, chose to become key players in Assam. Accordingly, the company annexed Lower Assam and made one Purander Singh the raja of Upper Assam. Mindful of the differences between the Ahoms and the tribes of Upper Assam, the British acknowledged the authority of the chiefs of the Moamarias, Khamtis, and Singphos over their respective communities and kept them out of the direct control of the new Ahom king.

At the recommendation of David Scott, Neufville was appointed political officer at Sadiya to engage the native hill tribes and ensure peace in the region. It was while operating in Upper Assam that the British came in contact with tribes like the Abors, Mishmis, Khamtis, Singphos, and others. With the integration of lower and central Assam into British territory the British had to engage the Bhutias, Akas, and Duflas inhabiting the northern side of Darrang District and also the Garos, Khasis, and Jaintias south of River Brahmaputra. After allowing Purander Singh to rule Upper Assam with restricted powers for a few years the company divested him of all powers in 1838 on charges of corruption and mismanagement.[19] Similarly, the hill region of Cachar, which was placed under Tularam, was absorbed by the British in 1854 on the pretext of the failure of Tularam's sons to put down the Naga raids and control the inter-tribal clashes.[20] Likewise, the British compelled the native kings of Manipur and Tripura to accept their supremacy. The British appointed political agents to supervise the working of the princely states and safeguard the colonial interests in the region. While engaging Manipur and Tripura the British came in touch with different tribal communities in the adjoining hills over which the princely states had some control.

Thus, by the middle of the nineteenth century the British had come in contact with almost all the hill tribes in the region. However, the colonial administration remained unclear as to what kind of policy to adopt to deal with the hill tribes. Initially, the authorities at the higher echelons of the British administration instructed their officers not to interfere in the internal affairs of the hill communities. But at the ground level tribal conflicts at times resulted in so much violence and bloodshed that the officers in the field were forced to intervene in different inter- or intra-tribal squabbles. Such engagements led to direct confrontations between the British subjects and the native tribes, to the disgust of the colonial authorities. The colonial policies of the British also played a part in intensifying conflicts between the British and the hill communities in the region.

Impact of British Rule on Hill Tribes of the Northeast

After the 1857 Sepoy Mutiny the company's rule came to an end with the British Crown deciding to take over direct control of the administration of India. The shift from company rule to the British Raj made little difference to the hill communities of northeast India as the Crown continued the same old policies of the company in the region. The colonizers' desire to increase revenues from their new possessions in the plains led the British to introduce certain changes in the region. Efforts were made to bring more and more land in Brahmaputra Valley under cultivation by initiating new forest and wasteland policies. British planters were allowed to expand tea cultivation up to the foothills. The British encouraged immigration of people from other regions to work for them in administration and in trade, agriculture and plantations in the region.

Such colonial policies in the plains had indirect effects on the hill areas of northeast India as well. The colonial government controlled the *duars* and the trade routes within – and to – other regions. British officers undertook surveys in the plains and hills with the idea of taking direct control over territories with mineral and forest resources. To facilitate the movement of their men, materials, and troops, the British constructed roads through the hills to connect the valley areas in the region with Bengal. On occasion, on the pretext of uniformity, the British began demanding tributes from the hill chiefs and imposed house tax and other taxes on some of the indigenous tribes. The right to *posa* that some of the hill tribes traditionally enjoyed was either denied or considerably restricted. Monetary transactions were introduced in place of the barter system. The hill communities, used to living autonomous lives, found it difficult to assimilate and accept the new changes. The presence of a large number of outsiders – whites and also people from the plains – in their midst or their vicinity caused fear and tensions among the hill people.

Colonial initiatives like enactment of new forest and wasteland policies, replacement of *posa* by payment in cash, abolition of slavery, expansion of tea plantations and agricultural activities up to the foothills, securing control over *duars* and markets, and so forth. Adversely affected the traditional sources of livelihood of the indigenous hill tribes. Some tribes felt the increasing burden of taxes and the growing administrative control over their traditional institutions and practices unbearable. Initially, when the British were not sure of their own strength they made treaties with the native rulers and chiefs treating them as equals. But once the colonial power consolidated its authority the old treaties that were based on mutual recognition and reciprocity were replaced by new treaties with more clauses and stringent conditions. The decisions to annex Jaintiapur (1835) and North Cachar Hills (1854) were taken to protect colonial interests. Such colonial interventions and policies that impinged upon the traditional rights of the indigenous people aggravated the hill tribes enough to attack British subjects and interests. Apart from handling acts of murder, plunder, and kidnapping that the Nagas, Lushais and other frontier tribes indulged in throughout the nineteenth century the British had to face several organized tribal revolts

H. SRIKANTH

and rebellions. To ward off threats to their colonial interests in the plains and to maintain peace along the borders the British followed the carrot-and-stick policy. Continuing with punitive expeditions wherever necessary, the British took up humanitarian measures to pacify the hill tribes of Assam.

Consolidation of British Rule in the Hills

The British knew from experience that the methods adopted to deal with native resistance elsewhere in India would not be of much use in dealing with the resistance of the hill tribes in northeast India. After muddling through several conflicts the British realized that as the nature of indigenous resistance differed from community to community they had to devise strategies appropriate to deal with each of the tribes. They found it easier to deal with the more civilized and less violent tribes such as the Khasis and Jaintias than with the wild tribes like the Nagas, Lushais, Garos, and Singphos. In the Khasi-Jaintia Hills, considering the hold that the traditional chiefs had over their people, conscious steps were taken through administrative interventions to diminish the powers of the chiefs and weaken the traditional institutions. The British took stern action against the Khasi chiefs that joined hands with U. Tirot Singh who rose in revolt against the British rule in 1829–30. After suppressing the revolt the British took possession of Mawsmai, Mawmluh, and Sohbar and appointed *sirdars* or headmen to carry on the day-to-day administration on behalf of the British government. The British claimed that they had rights to station troops, construct roads, and control trade and mining activities anywhere in the Khasi Hills. Yet, instead of annexing the entire Khasi Hills the British chose to restore the traditional authority of the chiefs and the *syiems* in the rest of the Khasi Hills and allowed them to handle civil and judicial matters in accordance with the native traditions – of course, on the condition that the traditional chiefs unconditionally accept the suzerainty of the British through treaties and *sanads*.[21]

Although civil administration in the Khasi States was thus left to the *syiems*, *lyngdohs*, *wahadadars* and *sirdars*, the British saw to it that matters relating to grave crimes, sedition and other issues of importance were directly dealt by the political agent appointed by the British. The political agent in charge of the Khasi-Jaintia Hills supervised and exercised considerable influence over the activities and functioning of the traditional chiefs. Theoretically, the areas under the *syiems* and other traditional chiefs were not part of British India. But in reality the British intervened in the functioning of the Khasi States by imposing unequal and discriminatory treaties and *sanads*. The British retained their control over the mines and roads and virtually dictated the rules to be followed with regard to succession of the *syiems* and many other administrative matters.[22] In the Jaintia Hills on the pretext of insubordination, the British compelled the Jaintia chief to relinquish his authority as king. Consequently, in 1835 the British annexed the plain areas of the Jaintia kingdom to Sylhet and placed the hills under the control of the political agent of the Khasi Hills who administered the Jaintia Hills with the help of *dollois* or *sirdars*.[23] Political control over the Jaintia Hills was further tightened after the Synteng Revolt in the 1860s. Similarly in the Garo Hills, overshadowing the traditional institutions of *noakmas*, the British appointed *laskars* and *zimmadars* from among the Garos to look after civil and criminal administration in the hills.[24]

H. SRIKANTH

The British took considerable interest in the administration of the hills inhabited by the Khasis, Jaintias, and Garos in view of their strategic location and commercial significance. But they followed an altogether different policy with regard to the frontier hills and other border areas. For some time the British were clueless as to how they should deal with the wild and barbaric frontier tribes, which they believed understood only the law of the jungle. In the beginning the British officers tried to lure the chiefs of Singpho, Naga, and Lushai communities to make treaties by offering presents, stipends, pensions, and land grants in the plains. But the British soon understood that it was difficult to get the frontier tribes to commit to any written treaties. The tribes did not understand the alien language and legal implications of the treaties, nor did they feel any need to show reverence to the treaties that they entered into with the white people.

The British made efforts to allay the fears of the hill communities by offering employment to tribes like the Thadous in tea plantations. But the hill communities were extremely individualistic and accepted no outside control or external domination. They tended to act on instinct and attacked people whom they perceived as enemies. Although the tribes had only primitive weapons, their hit-and-run guerrilla tactics caused considerable problems for the British authorities. To prevent the frontier tribes from plundering the villages and killing British subjects, the British undertook several punitive expeditions from time to time. For instance, to subdue the Mizo tribes the British sent expeditions in 1844, 1850, 1859, 1870–71 and 1889.[25] With the objective of creating terror in the minds of the defiant hill communities the British troops would destroy the villages and set fire to granaries. The British also sought cooperation from the kings of Manipur, Cachar, and Tripura to control the wild tribes, but in vain. Wherever possible the British tried to pit one indigenous tribal group against another, for example, the Khamptis against the Singphos and the Kukis against the Nagas. Denying access to *duars* and closing the *hats* were other means used by the colonial authorities to teach lessons to the rebels. The British raised different regiments such as the Rangpur Light Infantry, Assam Light Infantry, Gurkha Rifles, and Assam Rifles and stationed the troops in different places to deal with the defiant tribes.[26]

Inner Line Regulations: A Policy of Segregation?

The British learned from experience that the policies that appeared to be beneficial and profitable in the plains were often perceived by the hill tribes as threats to their existence. It became clear to the British that as long as encroachment of tribal lands by planters and cultivators continued it was impossible to ward off tribal attacks on British subjects and property. After gaining knowledge of the cultural and racial differences the British officials believed that the interests of the hill tribes and plainsmen were irreconcilable. In a way, all these factors contributed to the pursuit of the colonial policy of segregation through the enactment of the Inner Line Regulations in 1872–73. This Act gave powers to the lieutenant-governor to prescribe a line, "the Inner Line," in the frontier districts beyond which no British subject or foreign resident could pass without a license. The pass or license, even when given, would be subject to such conditions as would appear necessary. The regulations prescribed rules regarding trade, possession of land and other matters. Planters, Indians and British were not allowed to acquire land beyond the Inner Line either from the government or from any local chief

H. SRIKANTH

or tribe. It was left to the authorities to decide as to what part of the district would come under the regulations.[27]

The Inner Line Regulations were invoked in the North-East Frontier Tracts of Sadiya, Balipara, and Lakhimpur and in the Naga and Lushai Hills. The British only administered politically in the areas coming under the Inner Line. Later, following the Scheduled District Act of 1874 the frontier areas were exempted from the normal administrative procedures and legal codes applicable to other parts of the country. Instead of imposing direct rule, the British considered it wise to use the services of traditional tribal chiefs to consolidate their hold over the frontier tribes. To mediate between the conflicting tribes and communicate with them the British created the office of *dubashis* in the Naga Hills and of circle interpreters in the Mizo Hills. Administrative arrangements were devised such that the ordinary tribal people need not encounter British officers like the deputy commissioner and sub-divisional officers for day-to-day needs,[28] who intervened only in extreme cases involving murder and sedition. Though such regulations and Acts set limits to the jurisdiction of the civil officers and gave considerable internal autonomy to the native tribes in the frontier hills, the colonial authorities made it clear that the Inner Line should not be construed as the border. The British government always reserved the right to intervene militarily even in the territories coming under the Inner Line at any time to establish its authority and to maintain law and order.[29]

The policy of segregation pursued through the Inner Line Regulations helped the colonial administration in different ways. By halting the encroachment of tribal lands, pursuing the policy of least interference, and allowing the hill tribes to govern themselves in accordance with their own traditions and customs the British created a sense of security among the hill tribes and contributed to mitigation of tensions between the frontier tribes and the plainsmen. The policy relieved the British of the burden of setting up and running highly structured legal and administrative institutions in economically and socially underdeveloped areas. By making the tribes settle down in particular hills and restricting their movements into the plains the British made the tribes feel that they belonged to the hills and the hills belonged to them. Later, this policy of segregation helped the British in keeping the frontier tribes away from the influence of the Indian national movement. By precluding even positive interactions with the people of the rest of India the Inner Line policy helped the British officials, anthropologists and Christian missionaries make the hill tribes feel that racially, culturally, and historically they had nothing to do with the rest of India and with Indians.

It is essential to state here that the Inner Line Regulations were not invoked in all the hill areas of Assam. The British took direct control of the administration of the Garo and Jaintia Hills. In the Khasi Hills they took control of 31 villages and left other areas under the control of traditional chiefs. For many years Cherrapunji in the Khasi Hills used to be the center of British civil and military authority in the hills. Later, in 1861 the deputy commissioner's establishment in the Khasi Hills was shifted to Shillong town, which the British built by acquiring land from the *syiem* of Milliem. Shillong became the capital of Assam after it became a chief commissionership in 1874. Being the provincial capital of Assam several Bengalese, Assamese and Marwaris came and settled in Shillong as bureaucrats, professionals and businessmen. Because of Shillong's status the British refrained from imposing Inner Line Regulations in the Khasi-Jaintia Hills. Similarly, the

Garo Hills, being surrounded by the settled economy, were also found unsuitable for extending the Inner Line Regulations. Although from the point of view of social and economic development the Garo Hills were no different from the frontier hills the British officers chose not to invoke the Inner Line here as they felt it would disturb the ongoing trade between the Garo Hills and the adjoining plains.[30] Because of non-imposition of the Inner Line in the hills inhabited by native communities like the Khasis, Jaintias, and Garos both positive and negative interactions did take place between the native hill tribes and the immigrant non-tribal people. The native tribes inhabiting these hill areas, especially the educated among them, kept themselves abreast of the political developments and movements taking shape in the rest of India. Because of these reasons, although ethnic identities developed among the Khasis, Jaintias, and Garos also, they did not take an anti-Indian color at any time. This is true even in the case of Karbi-Anglong and the North Cachar Hills wherein the native tribes had close interactions with the valley people of Assam.

Colonial Administration in the Hill Areas

After occupying the valley areas of Assam the company created the office of commissioner and appointed a principal assistant in each district to take care of civil and criminal administration. Apart from strengthening the revenue, judicial, and criminal administration, the British took initiatives to develop agriculture, tea plantations, communications, and trade and mining operations in the valley.[31] However, in hill areas inhabited by the native tribes the British had to move cautiously. Initially, the British appointed political agencies in some hill areas where they felt it necessary, and placed them under the charge of political

agents or political officers. In some cases the deputy commissioners of the adjacent valley districts were given additional charge as political agents or officers for some time.
After consolidating their authority some hill areas were
converted into districts and placed under the charge of
deputy commissioners or principal assistant commissioners.
The political agency at Cherrapunji ceased with the appointment of C. K. Hudson in 1854 as principal assistant
commissioner of the Khasi-Jaintia Hills District. After the
shifting of the administrative headquarters from Cherrapunji to Shillong in 1864 the district of Khasi-Jaintia Hills
was constituted and placed under the charge of a deputy
commissioner who also acted as political officer in charge of
the Khasi States. Garo Hills became a full-fledged district
under a deputy commissioner in 1869 with Tura as its headquarters. In 1867 the Naga Hills District came into existence with Samaguting bordering Nowgong District of
Assam as its headquarters. After successful expeditions in
Mozema and Kohima, the headquarters of the Naga Hills
District was shifted to Kohima in 1878.[32]

Recognizing the practical difficulties of the Bengal
government in looking after the administration of the hills
and valleys of Assam, the commissionership of Assam was
formed in 1874. Different hill districts that until then were
under the supervision of the lieutenant governor of Bengal
were merged with the commissionership of Assam. Although the British established hold over the Lushai Hills
by 1890 the southern part of the hills remained under the
Chittagong administration while the northern part came
under the Assam administration. In 1895 the South and
North Lushai Hills Districts were merged into one district
under the commissionership of Assam.[33] No efforts were
made to bring the hill areas north of River Brahmaputra
populated by tribes such as the Akas, Duflas, Khamtis,

Miris, and Singphos under a district administration. The Assam Frontier Tracts Regulation 1880 provided for excluding the frontier tracts in Assam from the operation of enactments in force therein and left administration of these hill tracts to the traditional chiefs. The Dibrugarh Frontier Tract was created in 1882. In 1914 the British reorganized these hill areas into the North-East Frontier Tracts of Sadiya, Balipara, and Lakhimpur.[34] Separate political officers were appointed for Sadiya and Balipara frontier tracts, but Lakhimpur tract was placed under the charge of the deputy commissioner of Lakhimpur. In 1943 the Tirap Frontier Tract was created by amalgamating some portions of Lakhimpur and Sadiya frontier tracts and placed under the charge of a separate political officer, who operated from Margherita. The political officers or deputy commissioner in charge of these tracts operated from the bordering towns in the valley districts. They followed the policy of least interference in the internal affairs of these tribes and intervened only when their colonial interests were threatened.

The organization of hill districts in the names of dominant native tribes inhabiting the region did not mean that all the areas inhabited by those particular tribes were included in the respective districts. The Khasi-Jaintia District did not include the "Khasi States," which were placed under the *syiems* and other traditional authorities. It included the whole of Jaintia Hills, 31 Khasi villages which were directly under the control of the British, and Shillong city and the adjoining cantonment areas. Similarly, the Naga Hills District initially included only the Angami, Ao, Lotha, and Sema tribal areas. It was only in course of time that some other Naga tribal areas such as Mokokchung, Zunheboto, and Phek were incorporated into the Naga Hills District. Still, there were many other Naga-inhabited areas which were either left unadministered or made part of

Manipur or Burma. Similarly, it was several years after the constitution of the Garo Hills District that the British could bring the interior Garo tribes under the hold of the British administration. Likewise, the unadministered Lakher and Zongliang areas became part of the Lushai Hills District only in 1921 and 1931 respectively.[35]

Civilizing Mission:
Education and Christianity in the Hills

British officers like David Scott, Maj Jenkins and James Johnstone who worked for several years in the region realized that the hill tribes could not be tamed by treaties, punitive expeditions or material concessions. They felt that as long as the hill tribes remained backward and uncivilized it would be difficult for the British to make them accept the changes brought in by colonial rule. Hence, they considered it necessary to 'civilize' and 'humanize' the hill communities through the spread of modern education and Christianity. David Scott, the first agent to the governor-general for the North-East Frontier of Bengal experimented with his ideas in the Garo Hills by starting a school at Singamari in 1831 with the help of the Serampore Baptist Mission. Lord Amherst, the governor-general then, also supported the idea of spreading Christianity among the hill tribes. However, the directors of the East India Company in London, who subscribed to the policy of religious neutrality, disapproved of the initiatives taken in the Garo Hills. They were concerned that religious intervention may provoke the natives to revolt against the colonial rule. However, Scott argued that the hill tribes of the northeast were different from the Hindus and the Muslims in mainland India. He maintained that as the hill communities did not belong to any institutionalized religion the introduc-

H. SRIKANTH

tion of Christianity would not have any adverse reaction in the hills. Moreover, he justified taking help from the missionaries on the ground that it was meant for education and humanitarian purposes. Scott wanted to impart knowledge of agriculture and mechanical arts to the hill tribes so that they could become self-reliant.[36]

Maj Jenkins, who succeeded David Scott as agent to the governor-general of the North-East Frontier, believed that it was necessary to encourage Christian missionaries to carry on their activities in the hills to tackle internecine strife among the warring tribes. But by then, Serampore Mission abandoned its activities in Assam and the Khasi Hills due to financial constraints and inadequacy of manpower.[37] Hence Jenkins took the initiative to invite the American Baptist Mission Foreign Society to undertake a "mission of civilization among the warlike tribes." At the request of Jenkins, Rev. Nathan Brown of the American Baptist Mission started a school at Golpara for Garo boys. The government undertook to pay the maintenance expenses of the boys and salaries of the teachers and gave grants for preparation and printing of textbooks. Schools were established in Rongjuli, Damra, and Rajasimla. Rev. and Mrs Stodard played very important roles in the spread of education and Christianity among the Garos. The Roman Catholic Mission and the Seventh Day Adventists entered the Garo Hills in the 1930s and 1940s. Government-aided missionary schools were started in the northern part while the government directly undertook the responsibility of starting schools in the southern Garo Hills. The schools initially provided education through the Bengali medium. The missionaries developed the Garo dialect into a written language using the Bengali script. Later the missionaries started making use of the Roman script for the Garo language and began teaching the Garos in the Garo medium. They translated the Bible and other religious tracts, wrote textbooks and published Garo journals. With the help of the Garos educated in their schools the Church carried on evangelical work in the Garo villages. By bringing the Garos of different areas and clans to schools and to the Church British rule brought some kind of unity and understanding among the tribes.[38]

The Serampore Mission started educational activities and evangelical work in the Khasi Hills with the encouragement and protection of the local British officers. Krishna Pal of the Serampore Mission baptized the first Khasis in the foothills village of Pandua in 1813. The mission made efforts to translate the Bible into the Khasi language using the Bengali script. In addition to the school in Gauhati (now Guwahati) situated opposite the Pandua Hills, schools were started in Cherrapunji, Mawsmai, and Mawmluh. However, the Serampore Mission abandoned its activities in the Khasi Hills in 1838 because of its own internal problems. The Welsh Presbyterian Mission entered the Khasi-Jaintia Hills in 1841 and was the first to establish a church in the Khasi Hills. The mission baptized several Khasis and Jaintias, including those belonging to the ruling families. They started several schools and churches and provided medical services to the people in different Khasi states. At the end of the nineteenth century the Roman Catholic Mission also started activities in the Khasi-Jaintia Hills. They concentrated on educational and medical activities in Shillong. The Salesians of Don Bosco started schools and colleges in the early part of the twentieth century. During the devastating earthquake that hit the Khasi-Jaintia Hills in 1897, the missionaries undertook relief measures to help the victims. Thereafter, several local people converted to Christianity. The educated among them became pastors and played a key role in spreading the Christian

H. SRIKANTH

faith among their community. Some among them like Rev. Nichols Roy, Rev. Joseph Dhkar, and Rev. Mon Lyngdoh started indigenous churches such as the Church of God movement, the Assembly Church of Jesus Christ, and the Christ National Church.[39]

Maj Jenkins invited Rev. Bronson of the American Baptist Mission, who was working then among the Singphos. Bronson dared to reside in the midst of the Angami Nagas and started a school and a church at Namsang for the young and the old. Initially, because of their untamed habits and lack of time-consciousness, the tribes found it difficult to adjust to the school rules and discipline. Apart from teaching the three Rs, Bronson sought to impart lessons in industrial arts to the tribesmen. He asked the government to offer them facilities for improving the production of tea and salt. Despite the British government's hesitation to deviate from its self-declared policy of religious neutrality, for practical reasons the officers at the grassroots level supported the activities of Bronson. But Bronson, despite his enthusiasm and commitment, had to leave Namsang for health reasons. Rev. E. W. Clark came later and worked in the Ao-inhabited areas. Because of Inner Line regulations, the British authorities permitted him to find a settlement among the Nagas at his own risk with no assurance of protection from the British.[40] With the help of Godhula Brown, an Assamese convert, Clark started church and educational activities among the Ao Nagas. Later, Rev. C. D. King and still later Rev. Rivenburg and Mrs Rivenburg undertook missionary activities among the Angami Nagas. The Roman Catholic Mission made its entry into the Naga Hills in 1915.[41]

With the support of British officers, J. H. Lorrain and F. W. Savidge of the Arthington Mission started missionary activities in the northern Lushai Hills. They developed a script and grammar for the Lushai dialect, designed school primers and provided education and medical help. Later, Rev. D. Jones, Edwin Rowlands and Peter Fraser of the Welsh Presbyterian Mission took up missionary activities in the North Lushai Hills. J. Shakespeare, superintendent of the North Lushai Hills District, acknowledged the work of the missionaries in the pacification of the Lushais. In the South Lushai Hills District the British Baptist Missionary Society started its activities with the help of J. H. Lorraine and F. W. Savidge who had by then left the Arthington Mission. Later, the British government permitted the Roman Catholics and the Salvation Army to work in the Lushai Hills.[42]

Christian missionaries played a very important role in restoring peace in the region by pacifying the tribes and making them accept the changes introduced by British rule. What the colonial power could not do with its military might, the missionaries accomplished through the spread of education and Christianity. In course of their civilization-cum-humanitarian mission among the hill tribes, the missionaries encountered considerable hostilities and hardships. They had to demonstrate patience and tact in making the tribal people attend the schools and accept Christianity. Initially, some tribes looked at the missionary activities with suspicion and even hatred. A couple of missionaries working among the wild tribes were even hacked to death. Despite such reactions, the Christian missionaries continued their activities in different hill areas of northeast India. Apart from education, the missionaries provided medical services to the sick, taught the tribal peoples the value of hard work, personal hygiene and sanitation, and trained them in skills such as agriculture, horticulture, masonry, and carpentry.

In pursuit of their goals, the missionaries denounced several obnoxious and superstitious cultural and religious practices of the native tribes and encouraged the natives to give up their traditional ways of life by acquiring attitudes, values and behavior compatible with Christian and modernist values.[43] Although the missionaries sought material and monetary support from the colonial authorities, there were instances when the missionaries went ahead with their activities without their support and even dared to confront the colonial authorities on issues such as the practice of slavery among the hill communities.[44] Such instances could not, however, hide the shared ideological commonalities between the colonial authorities and the missionaries. The missionaries operated or were allowed to operate only in those hills where colonial interests so demanded. The humanitarian activities undertaken by the missionaries were to a considerable extent supported by the finances provided by the British government. The missionaries worked in the hills inhabited by the Khasis, Jaintias, Nagas, Mizos, and Garos. But they were conspicuous by their absence in the North-Eastern Hill Tracts and also in the Mikir Hills and North Cachar Hills where the British did not feel the need for missionary activities. Both the colonizers and missionaries looked at the hill tribes as wild savages who needed to be civilized and humanized in the Western, Christian mould. Both aspired to ensure that the hill communities reconciled to the changes introduced by the British and accept colonial rule.

One could see such overlapping consensus and identity of interests between colonialism and the missionaries even in countries like Canada, Australia and the US. Yet, it should be admitted that the missionaries who operated in northeast India did not imitate their counterparts in countries like the US and Canada where the missionaries, in the name of education and the mission of civilizing, separated children from their natural environment and put them in residential schools with the avowed purpose of alienating them from their native culture, language, and traditions, as well as abusing the native children physically, psychologically, and even sexually.[45] Contrary to what the missionaries did in Canada and the US, the missionaries in northeast India identified themselves with the region and the people. They learnt the local dialects of the hill tribes, developed scripts and wrote primers and books in the local languages. They started schools in villages and taught the students in their own languages. Although the spread of Christianity brought in certain changes in the native traditions and culture, many missionaries did not force the natives to give up practicing some of their age-old customs and traditions. Although the Synteng mutiny led by Okiang Nongba in the Jaintia Hills (1860–64), Sambudhan's revolt in the North Cachar Hills (1881–82), the Zeliangrong rebellion led by Jadonang and Gaidiliu in the Naga-inhabited areas of Manipur (1930–32), and the Seng Khasi movement that took place in the Khasi-Jaintia Hills during the 1930s had anti-Christian overtones,[46] it should be mentioned that on the whole the native hill communities of northeast India did not experience the extent of alienation that the indigenous people had experienced elsewhere following the spread of Christianity. Whatever might have been their initial reactions, in course of time the native hill communities began to consider the missionaries as benefactors.

Developments on the Eve of India's Independence

By the beginning of the twentieth century, partly because of its own efforts and partly due to missionary activities, the British had consolidated their authority in the hill areas adjoining the plains of Assam. Although there were sporadic revolts, by and large the British succeeded in restoring peace and order in the region. After engaging in violent confrontations for about five decades the native hill tribes began reconciling themselves to the changes that had been thrust upon them and started exploring the possibilities of development within the constraints imposed by colonial rule. Factors like development of commodity relations, expansion of communications, development of local languages, growth of modern education, and the spread of Christianity initiated significant changes in the tribal societies. Although the traditional institutions and leadership were allowed to function in the hills, their significance began to wane under colonial influence. While the administrative measures compelled the native communities to settle down in particular areas, the schools and churches established by missionaries emerged as new places of public interactions among the tribes. The new bonds that emerged from these interactions contributed to the decline of clan identities and led to the development of broader tribal ethnic identities such as Nagas, Mizos, Khasis, and Garos.[47]

From within each of the tribes there developed a middle class, which had its base neither in land nor in business. This class comprised newly-educated members working in modern professions and closely associated with the Church. Access to modern education and interaction with British officials and missionaries gave them knowledge about the larger world and implanted new ideas and aspirations in them. This class, either in collaboration with the traditional chiefs (as was the case with the Nagas), or in confrontation with their own chiefs (as in the case of the Mizos), began to organize different sub-tribes and articulate the collective interests of their respective ethnic communities.[48] The newly-emerging ethnic elite started socio-cultural organizations for uplifting their communities and contributed considerably to the construction of ethnic identities by differentiating themselves from people in the plains and also from other ethnic communities. They played a key role in shaping the attitudes of their members to the political developments taking place in the subcontinent during the last three decades of British rule in India.

After the First World War the British government came out with the Act of 1919 which introduced a system of diarchy and made provision for legislative councils at provincial levels. Although all major concerns such as finance, industry, and defense remained reserved subjects, the provincial legislative councils were given limited powers over transferred subjects like local self-government, education, health, agriculture, and so forth. With Assam becoming a governor's province in 1921 a state legislative council also came into existence in the province. However, following official recognition of all hill areas of Assam as backward tracts, the legislative council of Assam could not exercise its jurisdiction over the hills. Only Shillong urban constituency enjoyed legal representation in the state legislative council. Some members nominated to represent certain hill areas played virtually no role in the legislative council. As per the law the central and provincial legislation could be applied in the hills only with approval of the governor-general or the governor, with modifications as may be suggested. Since the legislative council had no authority over the hills the council members from the valley often expressed their opposition to bear the expenditure involved in administration of the hill areas.[49]

During this period the hills witnessed the birth of many native associations of the emerging middle classes such as the Naga Club and the Young Mizo Association. When the Simon Commission was constituted to make rec-

H. SRIKANTH

ommendations for constitutional reforms to accommodate the growing national aspirations of Indians across the country, the Naga Club, with the support of British officials, submitted a memorandum to the Simon Commission requesting it to exclude the Nagas from the political processes taking shape in the country.[50] But this view of the Nagas was not shared by other hill communities. The hill tribes living in the North-Eastern Hill Tracts remained unaware of the political developments taking place in the Indian subcontinent. But many educated middle-class intellectuals of the Khasi-Jaintia Hills expressed their willingness to become part of the new constitutional arrangements. The British government had to take into consideration differences in the levels of political and educational development in the hills. Their realization that some hill areas were more developed than others led them to come up with proposals for reorganization of the hill areas. Accordingly, on the basis of indicators such as literacy and political development of the region, the Act of 1935 grouped the hills into two categories: excluded and partially excluded.

The frontier areas such as the North-East Frontier Tracts, the Mizo Hills, and the Naga Hills were declared as excluded areas, whereas the Khasi-Jaintia Hills, Garo Hills, Mikir, and North Cachar Hills were designated as partially excluded areas. Although there were differences over including the Garo Hills as a partially excluded area,[51] the classification continued to guide the British administration in the hills of composite Assam. The administration of excluded areas was placed under the charge of the governor of Assam, who, as the agent of the governor-general exercised direct control over the hills included in the list. The excluded areas were out of the purview of the Assam provincial legislature; they had no representation in the provincial legislature. However, the partially excluded areas had their representatives in the Assam legislature which had powers to make laws with respect to these hill areas, subject to the approval of the governor of Assam.

Legally, the governor had overriding powers even with respect to the partially excluded areas although he rarely exercised them in practice.[52] The Inner Line Regulations were not enforced in the partially excluded areas. The division of hills into excluded and partially excluded areas had contradictory effects on the subsequent political developments in the hills. In the excluded areas the natives lived isolated lives without any positive interaction with the people of the rest of India. Naturally, the ethnic elite in the frontier/border areas were hesitant to join the Indian Union. In the North-East Frontier Tracts, which were left unadministered, the native hill tribes virtually had no knowledge of the political developments taking place in the Indian subcontinent. In contrast, the native people and leaders in the partially excluded areas related themselves to the political processes shaping the subcontinent and showed their willingness to join the Indian Union.

Another spin-off of the Act of 1935 which had serious implications for the hill tribes in northeast India in the years to come was the decision to separate Burma from British India. For administrative reasons, the British demarcated the boundaries between India and Burma. The boundaries were drawn arbitrarily without taking into consideration the fact that different native tribes inhabited both sides of the border. This did not create much of a problem for the native tribes as long as the British rule continued both in India and Burma. Since the British left the hills on either side of the borders almost unadministered, the borders then did not obstruct the normal lives of the hill communities. But after the Second World War when the British withdrew from both India and Burma, the fate of the hill tribes like the Nagas and Kukis living on both sides of the border was left to the mercy of the new nation states that came into existence.

Similar problems arose when British India was partitioned into India and Pakistan and some of the plains areas inhabited by the hill tribes such as the Khasis, Jaintias, and Garos became part of East Pakistan. Anticipating such problems, some British officials like J. H. Hutton, N. E. Parry and Robert Reid had proposed the idea of establishing a Crown Colony comprising all the hill districts/tracts of northeast India and Burma. As they believed that the hill communities had little to do with the Indians of the mainland India, the officers concluded that the creation of a Crown Colony was the only way to protect the backward native tribes from possible domination and neglect by the new rulers who were about to take over power in British India and Burma. The proposal could not make headway as it did not receive any attention or support by any of the parties involved in the negotiations for transfer of power at that point of time.[53]

The Second World War had virtually brought the Japanese forces to the backyard of the hills of northeast India. Compelled by the war situation, the British sought the support and involvement of the native tribes in the war effort. The Nagas and Mizos responded positively and helped the British forces in different forms. However, the Kukis revolted against the British, refusing to join the British Army as a labor corps.[54] Some native tribes lent support to the Indian National Army led by Subhas Chandra Bose against the Allied forces. The British decision to leave India caused considerable worry among the hill communities and activated political forces within. Every hill community was concerned about its future in post-colonial India. However, their reactions to joining India were not uniform. The Naga National Council (NNC) took the extreme stand of demanding freedom for the Nagas and expressed their desire not to be part of India.[55] But in the Mizo Hills which also happened to be an excluded area, the people were clearly divided. While the Mizo Union, representing the radical educated sections opposed to the traditional Mizo chiefs showed their willingness to join India, the Mizo chiefs toyed with the idea of joining other Mizo tribes in Burma and becoming independent.[56] In the Khasi Hills the majority of the *syiems* were in favor of joining India, but expected the Khasi States to be treated as other princely states and that their relationship with the province of Assam be determined by agreements.[57] There was no visible opposition in the Garo Hills, North Cachar Hills, and Mikir Hills to joining India and becoming part of Assam province.

With the British deciding to grant freedom to India the Indian nationalists established a Constitutional Assembly in 1946 for drafting a constitution for independent India. The Constitutional Assembly set up an Advisory Committee on Minorities and Tribal Areas under the chairmanship of Vallabhai Patel. Realizing the specificity of hill areas of the northeast, a subcommittee on the northeastern tribal areas and the excluded and partially excluded areas was constituted as part of the Advisory Committee under the chairmanship of Gopinath Bordoloi to suggest the appropriate institutional set-up for the hill districts. The subcommittee included some representatives of the hill communities as members and co-opted members. The committee received memoranda from the representatives of different hill communities. Bordoloi met the leaders of different hill communities and tried to convince them that their interests would be protected in independent India. The Naga National Council (NNC) boycotted the committee while the Mizo Union sent its representatives as co-opted members. The committee in its recommendations suggested the need for a special set-up for the tribal areas so that the tribal people could overcome the fear of exploitation or domination by the advanced sections of people from the plains. To make the native tribes overcome their apprehensions, the committee recommended that the hill tribes be allowed to enjoy full freedom in respect of their own manners, customs, inheritance, social organizations, and village administration. The Bordoloi Committee's recommendations took the shape of the Sixth Schedule of the Indian Constitution which made provision for Autonomous District Councils (ADCs) in all the hill districts of Assam. Only the Nagas rejected the proposal right at the outset, whereas other hill communities started a new journey in pursuit of greater autonomy and self-reliance within the Indian Union.

Conclusion

The British policy in the hill areas of composite Assam was quite different from what it was in the tribal areas of mainland India. Considering their geographic and strategic locations, the British did not feel the need for elaborate administrative arrangements for the hill communities. Protecting the borders and maintenance of law and order being the main concerns of the colonial administration in the hill districts/tracts, the British chose not to antagonize the indigenous communities as far as possible. Hence, they tried to co-opt the traditional chiefs wherever they felt necessary and left the day-to-day administration to the chiefs/local officers. As such, there was little uniformity in the structures and functions of local administration in the hills during the British rule. As the British refrained from taking over and exploiting the traditional sources of livelihood like land, forests, and other natural resources they could avoid confrontations with the indigenous communities.

The Christian missionaries also helped in mitigating tribal antagonism toward British colonial rule by winning over the indigenous communities through education and philanthropic activities. Emergence of educated middle classes from within the tribal communities led to the rise of native organizations which sought to unite related cultural and linguistic groups into ethnic communities. Political isolation of the hill peoples from the people of mainland India during the colonial regime had created a feeling of general mistrust against all non-tribal communities in them. Hence, some hill communities had some reservations against joining the Indian Union. But the hill communities then had few options to choose their own destinies. Although prior to the British colonization these areas were never under the control of any kings or emperors who ruled mainland India, after India became independent the hill communities had to become part of the Indian Union that sought to build a sovereign nation state. The Constitution of India no doubt took cognizance of the historic specificity of these hill districts/tracts, but the avowed intention of the Indian nationalist elite to bring the hill communities into the national mainstream brought the indigenous communities of the region into direct interface with the modern state as never before. Although unprepared and undecided, the hill communities had to start a new journey of uncertainties as peripheral constituents of an emerging liberal democratic nation state.

Notes and References

1. Irfan Habib, *Essays in Indian History: Towards a Marxist Perception* (New Delhi: Tulika Publishers, 1995), 231.
2. Michael H. Fisher, ed., *The Politics of the British Annexation of India, 1757–1857* (New Delhi: Oxford University Press, 1993), 59–93.
3. Christopher von Furer Haimendorf, "Aboriginal Rebellions in Deccan," *Man in India* 25:4 (December 1945), 208-216; Prakash Chandra Jain, *Social Movements among Tribals* (Jaipur: Rawat Publishers, 1994), 26–55.
4. Alexander Mackenzie, *The North-East Frontier of India* (New Delhi: Mittal Publications, 1994), 1.
5. H. K, Barpujari, *Problem of the Hill Tribes North-East Frontier, Vol. I* (Shillong: North-Eastern University Publications, 1998), 1–13.
6. Edward Tuite Dalton, *Descriptive Ethnology of Bengal* (New Delhi: Cosmo Publications, 1973), 1–73.
7. Barpujari, *Problem of the Hill Tribes*, 11–12.
8. J. B. Bhattacharjee, *Social and Political Formation: Pre-colonial North-East India* (New Delhi: Har-Anand Publications, 1991), 129–75.
9. Julian Jacobs, *The Nagas: Hill Peoples of Northeast India* (New York: Thames and Hudson, 1990), 69–76; I. Atola Changkiri, *The Angami Nagas and the British, 1832–1947* (Guwahati: Spectrum Publications, 1999), 13–14.
10. R. S. Lyngdoh, *Government and Politics in Meghalaya* (New Delhi: Sanchar Publishing, 1996), 136–50.
11. Jacobs, *The Nagas*, 33–5; Sajal Nag, *Contesting Marginalities: Ethnicity, Insurgency and Subnationalism in North-East India* (New Delhi: Manohar Publishers, 2002), 30.
12. Barpujari, *Problem of the Hill Tribes*, 13–14.
13. Nag, *Contesting Marginalities*, 29–31, 41–2.
14. Barpujari, *Problem of the Hill Tribes*, 16–18; Mackenzie, *North-East Frontier*, 21.

15. *Our Native Peoples –: Nootka* (Victoria: British Columbia Heritage Series 1, 1996), 47.

16. H. K. Barpujari, *Assam in the Days of the Company* (Shillong: North-Eastern University Publications, 1996), 39–40.

17. Barpujari, *Problem of the Hill Tribes*, 27–8.

18. Edward Gait, *A History of Assam* (Guwahati: Lawyer's Book Stall, 1992), 278.

19. Barpujari, *Assam*, 133–41.

20. Gait, *History of Assam*, 289–95.

21. Barpujari, *Problem of the Hill Tribes*, 64.

22. Helen Giri, *The Khasis under British Rule* (New Delhi: Regency Publications, 1998), 120–35.

23. D. R. Syiemlieh, *British Administration in Meghalaya: Policy and Pattern* (New Delhi: Heritage Publishers, 1989), 73.

24. J. B. Bhattacharjee, *The Garos and the English, 1865–1874* (New Delhi: Radiant Publishers, 1978), 182–201.

25. Amiresh Ray, *Mizoram* (New Delhi: Regency Publications, 1998), 120–35.

26. Barpujari, *Problem of the Hill Tribes*, 42–3.

27. Mackenzie, *North-East Frontier*, 55–6; Nag, *Contesting Marginalities*, 47.

28. Piketo Sema, *British Policy and Administration in Nagaland, 1881–1947* (New Delhi: Scholar Publications, 1992), 29–36; Ray, *Mizoram*, 147–8.

29. J. N. Chowdhury, *Arunachal Pradesh: From Frontier Tracts to Union Territory* (New Delhi: Cosmo Publications, 1983), 230.

30. Syiemlieh, *British Administration*, 142–3.

31. Barpujari, *Assam* , 234–65.

32. Changkiri, *Angami Nagas*, 112.

33. Robert Reid, *History of the Frontier Areas Bordering Assam, 1883–1941* (Delhi: Eastern Publishing House, 1983), 37–44.

34. Chowdhury, *Arunachal Pradesh*, 230–5.

35. Sema, *British Policy*, 22–8; J. B. Bhattacharjee, *The Garos and the English, 1865–1874*, 55–7; Ray, *Mizoram*, 44.

36. N. K. Barooah, *David Scott in North-East India: A Study in British Paternalism* (New Delhi: Munshiram Manoharlal, 1970), 185–95.

98   H. SRIKANTH

37. Lal Dena, *Christian Missions and Colonialism: A Study of Mission-ary Movement in North East India with Particular Reference to Manipur and Lushai Hills, 1894–1947* (Shillong: Vendrame Institute, 1988), 21.
38. P. C. Kar, *The Garos in Transition* (New Delhi: Cosmo Publications, 1983), 70–87.
39. O. L. Snaitang, *Christianity and Social Change in Northeast India* (Shillong: Vendrame Institute, 1983), 65–95.
40. Dena, *Christian Missions*, 26.
41. Changkiri, *Angami Nagas*, 176–79.
42. Dena, *Christian Missions*, 47; Ray, *Mizoram*, 133–8.
43. Snaitang, *Christianity*, 181–3.
44. Dena, *Christian Missions*, 65–81.
45. Robert J. Muckle, *The First Nations of British Columbia: An Anthropological Survey* (Vancouver: UBC Press, 1998), 68–9.
46. H. K. Barpujari, *Problem of the Hill Tribes North East Frontier, Vol. II* (Shillong: North-Eastern University Publications, 1998), 78–9; also Mackenzie, *North-East Frontier*, 147–8; Jacobs, *Nagas*, 161–4; Syiemlieh, *British Administration*, 171–4.
47. Nag, *Contesting Marginalities*, 107.
48. Ibid., 59–60, 86–7; Syiemlieh, *British Administration*, 169–71, 178–80.
49. Lyngdoh, *Government and Politics*, 73–4.
50. V. K. Nuh, ed., *The Naga Chronicle* (New Delhi: Regency Publications, 2000), 111–12.
51. Lyngdoh, *Government and Politics*, 90–102.
52. Syiemlieh, *British Administration,*, 181–7.
53. Ibid., 188–93.
54. Sema, *British Policy*, 148–9; Ray, *Mizoram*, 150–1.
55. Nuh, *Naga Chronicle*, 63–4.
56. Nag, *Contesting Marginalities*, 107–20.
57. Lyngdoh, *Government and Politics*, 191.

H. Srikanth

4

TOWARD INDIAN SELF-GOVERNMENT IN BRITISH COLUMBIA: PROBLEMS AND PROGRESS

P rior to the colonization of North America by the European powers hundreds of FN communities inhabited the continent. With colonizers taking over control of their lands and destroying their traditional institutions, these politically autonomous and economically self-reliant communities lost their independence and became passive subjects of the alien rulers in their own territories. Unrestricted immigration, deceptive treaties, brutal repression, disease and deaths decimated and marginalized the native communities and compelled them to live within the restrictions of the reserves created for them. The formation of the Canadian federation in 1867 and adoption of liberal democratic institutions did not bring any significant change in the status of FN communities in Canada. In 1876 the Canadian government passed the Indian Act to govern the status-Indian communities living on the reserves in Canada.[1] The Act put an end to traditional forms of governance by creating elected band governments on the reserves. It set aside reserve lands for the "use and benefit" of specific Indian bands. Title to the land, however, was held by the Crown, making the reserves pockets of federal jurisdiction within the provinces.

Under the terms of the Indian Act the Crown held the land title and only allowed the Indians to use and occupy them.² As such, no Indian band had the right to sell or dispose of reserve lands. The Act guaranteed to status-Indians: the right to reside on the reserve assigned to his or her band; freedom from estate and land taxes on reserve lands; freedom from income taxes on income earned on the reserve; and the right to vote in band council elections. The Indian Act delegated limited powers to the band councils to take decisions concerning the band affairs. However, the real powers continued to be in the hands of the ministers, superintendents and other officers appointed by the Canadian government. Under the Indian Act regime the FNs became wards to be protected and treated paternalistically by their 'benevolent' masters. The Indian Act did not allow the Indians to become self-sufficient and truly empowered. The band councils' powers to make bylaws were limited and regulated by the governor-in-council. The band councils had neither powers nor means to devise and implement their own policies and programs.³ Since the bands did not have any corporate status their ability to engage in economic developmental activities was considerably restricted. Further, the Act failed to delineate differences among the Indian communities and imposed uniform laws regulating the lives of FNs living on the reserves. It did not recognize the FN women who were married to non-Indians and the FNs who moved to the cities for a variety of reasons. The bands as such had no real powers to decide on who could be given membership. The Canadian government used the Indian Act to deny Canadian citizenship to the status-Indians and insisted on those who sought Canadian citizenship to give up the Indian status. Contrary to the Canadian government's claims the Act remained a piece of racist legislation and a symbol of discrimination.⁴

The policy of segregation pursued in Canada prevented mutual understanding and meaningful interactions

H. SRIKANTH

between the Indians and the Canadian citizens. By and large, the Canadian citizens showed little interest in understanding the plight of the FNs. Their outlook toward the natives remained racist. However, positive gestures made by the FNs during the Second World War helped in erasing to an extent stereotype images of the aboriginal people from the minds of the Euro-Canadians. Following the changes in the citizens' perceptions about the natives the government came under pressure to appoint a royal commission to revise the Indian Act and put an end to the discrimination that the FNs experienced for about a century. Responding positively to public opinion a joint committee of both the House of Commons and the Senate was set up in 1946 to review the Indian Act. Following its report a new Indian Act came into existence in 1951.

Several restrictive and antiquated clauses were deleted. The ministers' powers were considerably reduced and the band councils given more powers. Although assimilation as a goal was retained the clauses that aimed at aggressive civilizing and compulsory enfranchisement were given up. The federal government launched programs to promote community development and local government on the reserves. A nationwide program was undertaken to integrate the FN students into Euro-Canadian schools. A series of leadership training courses was organized to prepare the reserve communities to take greater part in managing their own affairs. Subsidization of several government programs led to definitive improvements in the socioeconomic conditions of FNs. With the federal government taking the lead and provinces following it, by the middle of the 1960s franchise rights were guaranteed to all FNs. As health services improved the declining trend in the Indian population was reversed. Many Indian children got access to secondary and post-secondary education.[5] All these changes gave rise to a new class of educated FNs who began to play key roles in organizing and channelizing the discontent of the native population for achieving the goal of self-government.

The 1951 amendments to the Indian Act and the changes in the governments' attitudes toward the FNs did not, however, bridge the divide between the Canadian citizens and FNs. Some discriminatory provisions like the ones that denied Indian status to native women married to non-natives were retained for another three decades. The Act continued to look at the band council as the basic unit of administration and as a result the bands failed to reap economies of scale to become self-sufficient. Band councils and Indian associations continued to depend primarily on the federal government for operational funding and political recognition. The Indian leaders were exposed to a daily diet of political pressure and bureaucratic resistance.[6] Band councils had few powers to plan and implement programs beneficial to them. The aboriginal people received services that had been conceived, regulated, and negotiated by the government and the service providers without any native inputs. As the designated beneficiaries of services, the aboriginals had no rights to comment on the quality, relevance, or method of provision of the services. Everything had already been agreed upon in their absence.[7] It is then natural that FNs felt suffocated under the Indian Act regime. Further, with the growth of the native population after 1945 the pressure on land and resources on the reserves increased, forcing the natives to look beyond the means and opportunities guaranteed by the Indian Act. The Indian situation in BC would throw more light on the changing status, problems, and dilemmas of the FNs.

FNs in British Columbia in the 1950s and 1960s

By the mid-twentieth century considerable changes did take place in the socioeconomic conditions of the native communities in BC. H. B. Hawthorn and C. S. Belshow's study on FNs in British Columbia (1958) threw considerable light on the transformation taking place within the FN communities. The study showed that although the natives continued to depend on domestic production – food-gathering, hunting, fishing – for a livelihood, they were also exposed to markets, store foods, modern gadgets, and new crops and fruit trees. A traditional background, clan leadership and potlatch were no longer the only determinants of wealth and status. Alongside increases in the per capita income, marked differences in income were observed among the Indian communities. During this period band membership was the basis for determining one's Indian status. The Indian Branch gave recognition to different types of band councils. While some had representative councils, several small bands were without a representative council of any kind. Unlike traditional Indian chiefs who held offices during competency, the chiefs and councilors in BC were elected for two years. On paper the Indian Act gave powers to the band councils the right to protest against alterations in band lists; admit Indians to band membership; allot land; grant timber-cutting licenses; cultivate unused land; dispose of non-mineral substances; adjust sale, lease, or lending contracts; spend capital and revenue monies; make bylaws for defined purposes of local government; and raise money by law.[8]

However, in reality these powers were restricted considerably, partly due to bureaucratic interference and partly because of dependence of band councils on federal finances. The band funds were held in Ottawa and the officials-in-charge of Indian affairs were extremely skeptical of the bands' ability to manage the funds meant for them. It was rightly pointed out that the whole framework of financial administration was designed to 'protect the Indian from himself' and the focus of administrative action was not education of the Indian but the manipulation of his property.[9] Moreover, since most bands were small and had little resources, even with government subsidies they could not become efficient administrative units capable of providing social services on an optimum scale. The FNs had no official channels to unite and pool the resources of different bands to ensure efficient administration. Further, most Indian reserves in BC remained small and underdeveloped. Unlike many other Canadian provinces which were covered under different federal Indian treaties, BC by and large remained a non-treaty province.[10] Of the total of 2,300 reserves in Canada, BC alone has around 1,600 although the average size is much smaller compared to the reserves in other provinces covered by federal treaties. Being small in size and deficient in resources the reserves were not in a position to accommodate any new members into the bands. During this period the Indians had only one elected representative in the legislative assembly of the province. They hardly had any role in the affairs of the government and political parties that made policies and programs for the benefit of the Indians. All these factors necessitated native political organizations which could effectively articulate the interests of FNs both at provincial and national levels.

In the 1950s the FN interests in BC were articulated by two FN organizations, namely, the Native Brotherhood of British Columbia (NBCC), and the North American Indian Brotherhood (NAIB).[11] With Protestantism as the unifying force, the NBCC founded by Alfred Adams and Peter Kelly organized tribal groups inhabiting the western, central, and northern coastal areas in BC. The NAIB started by Andrew Paull had its base on the south coast and the central and southern interior areas where Roman Catholics were predominant. Andrew Paull facilitated the formation of a Kamloops-based and Shuswap-supported organization called the Confederacy of the Interior Tribes of British Columbia. Despite their efforts such provincially-based Indian organizations could not make much headway in BC partly because of leadership crises and partly due to continuing tribal loyalties. More than territory-based Indian associations, Indians began to support tribe-based organizations. Frank Calder, a charismatic Nisga'a leader, formed the Nisga'a Tribal Council in 1955. Leaders like Jack Peter took initiative in the formation of the Nuu-chah-nulth Tribal Council in 1958. In 1964 the Southern Vancouver Island Tribal Federation (SVITF) came into existence to organize Coast Salish bands in the Cowichan agency on Southern Vancouver Island.[12] Alongside these tribe-based organizations the end of the 1960s witnessed the foundation of three more FN organizations: the Indian Homemakers' Association in 1968, the British Columbia Association of Non-Status Indians (BCANSI) and the Union of British Columbia Indian Chiefs (UBCIC) in 1969.[13]

Hawthorn Report: FNs as Citizens-Plus

Taking cognizance of the growing discontent among the FNs the federal government hired the services of Prof. Hawthorn in the 1960s to conduct an enquiry into the social, economic, and political conditions of the status-Indians and to make appropriate policy recommendations for improving their living conditions. The Hawthorn Committee report released in 1966 and 1967 criticized the policies of assimilation pursued by the Canadian governments

and exposed the pitiable state of FNs in Canada. The committee felt that most problems of the FNs resulted from the
neglect that had followed from their historical post-Con-
federation status as wards. Since non-aboriginal Canadians
built a prosperous society on the lands and resources orig-
inally owned by the aboriginals, the Hawthorn Committee
opined that Canada should treat the FNs as "Citizens-
Plus."[14] By "plus" the committee meant that apart from
guaranteeing the normal rights and duties of citizenship,
the Indians possess certain additional rights as charter members of the Canadian community. The committee thus
sought to preserve the native "difference" while simultane-
ously recommending common citizenship for the Indian
people and the majority population. The recommendations
of the Hawthorn Committee indeed made a breakthrough
in approaching the Indian question in Canada. But the
Canadian government paid little attention to the committee's observations and recommendations. Contrarily, a couple of years after the release of the Hawthorn Report the
federal government came out with a White Paper which
sought to eliminate Indian "difference" and assimilate all
the aboriginals into the Canadian mainstream.

The White Paper of 1969

Whatever might be its limitations, the Indian Act
recognized the FNs as indigenous communities. The FNs
took cognizance of the fact that the Act in a way helped
them preserve their identity as Indians, but at the same time
they never considered the Indian Act as representing their
true aspirations. In fact they contested the paternalistic and
assimilatory provisions of the Act and demanded recognition of aboriginal rights to land and governance. They complained of discrimination that the natives experienced at the

H. SRIKANTH

hands of the white racists in Canada and exposed how the Indian Act failed to protect them. Canadian governments' inducements to convert them into Canadian citizens never appealed to the FNs. More than the wish to be treated as equal citizens of Canada the FNs aspired for recognition of and respect for their unique histories. The aboriginal people envisioned themselves as standing apart from the Canadian society and enjoying a one-to-one relationship with the Crown in Canada. These apparent contradictions in the native perceptions and aspirations became more explicit in 1969 when the Canadian government headed by Prime Minister Trudeau came out with a document entitled, "Statement of the Government of Canada on Indian Policy," more widely known as the White Paper.

The White Paper proposed to put an end to the century-old Indian policy that perpetuated injustice and prevented the Indians from becoming full members of the Canadian community. According to it, "the separate legal status of Indians and the policies which have flowed from it have kept the Indian people apart from and behind other Canadians."[15] It argued that the plight of the Indians could be overcome by removal of discriminatory barriers and by opening up "doors of equal opportunity" to them. In order to achieve this goal the government proposed to repeal the Indian Act and recommended eventual abolition of the aboriginal rights and transfer of the responsibility of Indians to the provinces.[16] According to Trudeau, his government had only two choices: retaining the conventional way of administering the Indians by adding bricks of discrimination, or discarding the old system by giving Indians full status in society. In one of his speeches supporting the White Paper Trudeau remarked that it was "inconceivable that in a given society one section of society have a treaty with the other section of the society. We must be all equal under the laws and we must not sign treaties amongst ourselves." He contended that a liberal democracy cannot allow special rights for any community, for "we can't recognize aboriginal rights because no society can be built on historical 'might-have-beens'."[17]

What appeared to liberals like Trudeau a well-intentioned policy seeking an end to discrimination and ensuring equal status to the native communities in Canada appeared to the FNs as a ploy to destroy their Indian identity and deny them aboriginal rights. The White Paper was accused of everything from cultural genocide, to a policy of termination to callous expediency in offloading federal costs, and reneging on Crown responsibilities. The liberal logic of the White Paper received a comprehensive indigenous response in the Harold Cardinal – authored *Red Paper*. In his response he also gave vent to the aspirations and expectations of the Indian communities in Canada. Thus, the White Paper shook the Indian world and stirred up nationalist sentiments in it. It activated different dormant Indian organizations and gave birth to some new ones. The Union of British Columbia Indian Chiefs (UBCIC) representing about 190 chiefs of BC was formed in November 1969 in direct response to the White Paper. The National Indian Brotherhood (NIB) and Native Council of Canada (NCC) emerged as national-level organizations representing the interests of the registered Indians and non-status Indians, respectively. The White Paper controversy also gave birth to militant Indian groups, which called themselves Red Power. It is during this period that the FN communities began to identify themselves as First Nations. These native organizations played significant roles at provincial and national levels to articulate the Indian aspirations for self-determination and self-government. Due to their growing activism and stiff resistance the Canadian government was forced to retract its moves and look for alternative strategies to deal with the First Nations. The Supreme Court verdict in Calder's case involving the Nisga'a claim (1973) also compelled the federal government to rethink its Indian policies and programs.

The Calder Case: Recognition of Indian Title

The Nisga'a of Northern BC sought formal recognition of their aboriginal title on the pleas that they had been living on the land they presently occupied since time immemorial. Frank Calder, the founder and president of the Nisga'a Tribal Council maintained that his people's aboriginal title had never been extinguished, and that none of their territory had ever been ceded to Britain. After losing their case in the Supreme Court of British Columbia and the British Columbia Court of Appeals the case was taken to the Supreme Court of Canada. Although the Nisga'a legally lost the case even there, they won a moral victory with the majority of the judges acknowledging the existence of aboriginal rights. In the judgment Justice Wilfred Judson speaking for three judges held that the aboriginal rights which once existed were subsequently extinguished by pre-Confederation enactments. In contrast Justice Emmett Hall, speaking on behalf of three dissenting judges took the stand that the aboriginal title of the Nisga'a had never been lawfully extinguished and that this title could be asserted even today. With the seventh judge, Justice Louis-Philippe Pigeon holding against the Nisga'a on technical grounds, the majority decision tilted against the Nisga'a. Yet, the case became a landmark in the history of the aboriginal peoples' struggle in Canada for it disowned the *terra nullius* argument and acknowledged that Canada was inhabited by organized groups of Indians who had settled there several centuries before the white men 'discovered' the land. This was contrary to the position held by some of the judges, who argued that the Nisga'a were primitive people who had few institutions of the civilized world and were virtually oblivious of Western notions of private property.

Justice Hall stated in his judgment that on the eve of European contact the Nisga'a were a distinctive cultural entity with their own concepts of ownership indigenous to their culture and capable of articulation under the common law, having "developed their cultures to higher peaks in many respects than in any other part of the continent north of Mexico." He clearly stated in his verdict that the Nisga'as right to possession of the lands delineated and their right to enjoy the fruits of the soil of the forest, and of the rivers and streams within the boundaries of said lands had not been extinguished by the Province of British Columbia or by its predecessor, the colony of British Columbia, or by the governors of that colony.[18] Although the support of three judges was not enough for a legal victory the dissenting voice in the judgment was enough to persuade the liberal government of Trudeau to change its policy and acknowledge the need for starting negotiations with the Nisga'a. Other important court judgments that followed the Calder case, such as the Guerin case (1984), the Sparrow case (1990), and more recently the Delgamuukw case (1997) also affirmed Indian rights and expanded their meaning. The courts came out in support of aboriginal rights to control land and natural resources and intervened to regulate commercial fishing and logging activities when they seemed to disrupt traditional sources of livelihood for the Indians. In the Delgamuukw case the court entertained oral histories of the Indian communities as bases for Indian claims. All these court interventions compelled the BC government to reconsider its strategies with regard to the FNs.

Aboriginal Activism

After the withdrawal of the White Paper the National Indian Brotherhood (NIB) emerged as the representative of the status-Indians at the national level. Since the NIB did not take interest in the non-status Indians another organization named the Native Council of Canada (NCC) came into existence to work for the non-status Indians and Metis. This rift between status and non-status Indians continued at both the national and provincial level. In BC the UBCIC sought to represent the interests of the status-Indians through traditional tribal chiefs. It did not evince any interest in joining hands with organizations such as the British Columbia Association of Non-Status Indians (BCANSI). But in BC, as mentioned earlier, provincial- and national-level Indian organizations started losing their significance for different reasons and their place was filled in by different tribal organizations like the Nisga'a Tribal Council, the Nuu-chah-nulth Tribal Council, the South Vancouver Island Tribal Federation, and others representing the interests of different native tribal/linguistic groups. These tribal organizations chose to maintain their autonomy and were not willing to subordinate their interests to any provincial- or national-level Indian organizations. They rejected the twin principles – status/non-status differentiation, and rule by band councils – on which the Indian Act rested. They refused to confine their political activism to the reserves and did not accept the tribal chiefs as their natural leaders. Like the Nisga Tribal Council, most other tribal councils stood for popular sovereignty, linguistic group exclusiveness, status/non-status unity, band council's acquiescence to the tribal council, and pursuit of the land claims as the primary political tasks of the First Nations.[19]

The emergence and consolidation of tribal councils contained the growth of UBCIC. To regain its hold the UBCIC began to adopt militant tactics to project itself as the sole representative of the FNs in BC. The much-needed political platform for this was provided in the late 1970s by Trudeau's government which sought to bring in a new constitution for Canada. In one sense Canada's move to end its formal ties with the Crown and have its own constitution aroused fears among the aboriginal groups across Canada about their future. The First Nations rightly complained that the federal government did not seek their consent while seeking repatriation and that the Indian representatives were invited to the First Ministers' Conference only as observers, not as equal partners. They expressed fears that the new constitutional arrangements that the federal government was negotiating with the provincial governments would deprive them of even the limited concessions they had been enjoying under the Crown's laws. Their fears and apprehensions drove the national- and provincial-level aboriginal organizations to take to the streets to pressurize the governments to listen to them. Aboriginal organizations like the Assembly of First Nations (FN) and tribal organizations such as the Nisga'a Tribal Council were more interested in ensuring that their interests were protected in the new constitutional and political arrangements.

Contrarily, national and provincial organizations of tribal chiefs such as NIB and UBCIC tried militant strategies to halt the repatriation. Apart from moving the courts in Canada and abroad to seeking a judicial declaration that Indian consent was necessary before the constitution could be repatriated, the UBCIC mobilized thousands of Indians to Ottawa and to Great Britain in the name of a "Constitutional Express." Its representatives met political leaders in Britain and sought their support in stalling the repatriation process. All such pressures and militant postures from NIB, UBCIC and other provincial organizations of the tribal chiefs in Canada could not prevent the governments in Canada from going ahead with the constitutional process. But their resistance did help in ensuring that aboriginal rights were included as part of the new Canadian constitution. Accordingly, Section 25 of Canadian Charter of Rights and Freedoms guaranteed that the Charter would not abrogate or derogate any aboriginal treaty or other rights or freedoms pertaining to the aboriginal peoples of Canada. By designating the Indian, Metis, and Inuit as aboriginal peoples Section 35 clearly stated that the aboriginal and treaty rights of the aboriginal peoples of Canada were thereby recognized and affirmed.[20] The federal government also agreed to organize First Ministers' Conferences to negotiate with aboriginal leaders in accommodating their aspirations for self-government.

From First Ministers' Conference to Charlottetown Accord

After the enactment of the Constitution Act of 1982 the national- and provincial-level Indian organizations continued to exercise political, moral, and intellectual pressure on the Canadian government to acknowledge their right to self-government. It was during this period that the term First Nations virtually replaced the earlier representations of FN communities as bands. In the three First Ministers' Aboriginal Constitutional Conferences held between 1983 and 1987 the aboriginal organizations tried to pressurize the federal and provincial governments to agree in principle to the idea of Indian self-government. The conferences, however, failed to arrive at any decision, as four provinces including BC insisted on clarifying the meaning of self-government first before they were asked to grant it.[21] When the same governments which expressed their opposition to Indian self-government showed eagerness to appease Quebec in the Meech Lake Accord, which sought to give recognition to Quebec as a distinct entity,[22] the native groups criticized the double standards of the Canadian leaders. The aboriginal leaders articulated their concerns and helped block the passage of the Meech Lake Accord in 1990, much to the pleasure of many First Nations people and other Canadians who opposed the accord for a variety of reasons.[23] The failure of Meech Lake compelled the Canadian government to follow up new constitutional talks with aboriginal groups and conclude the Charlottetown Accord. Although the Charlottetown Accord was defeated in the referendum held in 1992 the natives continued to look at the agreement with pride, for it was during these talks that the Indian leaders were treated with respect as equal partners in the negotiations. The Charlottetown Accord was also important as the government officially recognized self-government as an inherent right of the aboriginal peoples.

Penner Committee Report of 1983

On the eve of the initial First Ministers' Aboriginal Constitutional Conference in 1983 a Special Committee on Indian Self-Government was appointed by the House of Commons under the chairmanship of Keith Penner. In its report the Penner Committee pointed to the difficulties inherent in pursuing devolution policies within the parameters of the Indian Act. The Penner Report also endorsed the Indians' demands for creation of First Nations Governments as distinct political and administrative entities which would be linked but not subordinated to federal and provincial governments. The committee recognized the need for a new relationship based on constitutional recognition of First Nations governments as a distinct order of government in Canada.[24] The committee felt that education, child welfare, and health care could be placed under the jurisdiction of the Indian governments for design, implementation, and administration of delivery systems, programs, and services. It sought special enabling legislation to set out general principles under which Indian governments would be developed. The committee encouraged the ongoing bilateral and treaty-making processes.

With respect to the structures and powers of Indian governments in Canada, the Penner Committee felt that although the primary political unit of Indian government must continue to be the band, self-government arrangements should accommodate situations where First Nations might choose to come together on different bases for various purposes. Further, the committee felt that the structures of government and systems of accountability needed to be chosen by First Nations members themselves. The nature and scope of their powers and jurisdictional fields should be identified and arrived at through negotiated agreements. Areas of jurisdictional overlap between governments and First Nations may be subject to joint control and authority. The report recognized the economic disadvantages of reserve communities and called upon federal authorities to upgrade the socioeconomic infrastructure of the band communities. Adequate land and resource base, settlement of claims, and correction of deficiencies in community infrastructure were rightly identified as essential preconditions for Indian self-government. The committee proposed alternative and flexible funding methods and arrangements for Indian self-government. In the Penner Committee model, the notion of Citizen-Plus implied that while Indians would be entitled to all the benefits and associated responsibilities of Canadian citizenship, Indian governments could selectively choose to exempt their people from some of the unwanted constraints of Canadian citizenship such as the Charter of Rights and Freedoms.[25] In subsequent years the Penner Report substantially influenced Canadian Indian policy.

Struggles for Indian Self-Government

Ever since FNs started organizing themselves politically for protection of their aboriginal identities and rights they have been demanding Indian self-government. Beginning in 1951 the Canadian government started promising some form of self-government for the Indian communities, but there was no consensus as to what one would actually mean by self-government. Initially, the federal government was ready to grant only municipal-type powers to Indian self-governments. On the other extreme there were some radical Indian groups in Canada which interpreted self-governments as something synonymous with sovereign governments and demanded a complete break with white Canada. But the majority of First Nations in Canada realized that because of historical, demographic, and territorial disadvantages and also due to ethnic divisions within, it was just not possible to dream of sovereign FN states. The historic Dene Declaration of 1975, passed by a joint assembly of the Indian Brotherhood of the Northwest Territories and the Metis Association, which put declared self-determination, nationhood, and territoriality within the bounds of Canada as the objectives, rightly reflected the aspirations of the majority of First Nations in Canada.[26] But differences persisted among the Indian communities and organizations as to what powers and material requirements were indispensable for genuine Indian self-governments. In view of

118   H. SRIKANTH

the differences and disparities in interests, capabilities, and aspirations across the Indian communities, it was just not possible to arrive at a consensus as to what would be meant by Indian self-government. Depending on what they considered to be indispensable for their interests each tribe or group of tribes began searching for appropriate structures and forms of self-government suited to them. In return for the land surrendered, the Cree and Naskapi Indian nations of Northern Quebec received a cash award amounting to hundreds of millions of dollars through the James Bay and Northern Quebec Agreement concluded in 1975. They were also given tracts of community lands with exclusive hunting and trapping rights over large areas. In addition the agreement made provision for introduction of new systems of local governance on lands set aside for their use.

These agreements paved the way for the Cree-Naskapi (of Quebec) Act. Passed in 1984, it was the first aboriginal self-government legislation in Canada.[27] In the province of BC the first modern experiment to replace the Indian Act with community government and self-management took place on the Sechelt Reserve located beside Sechelt town. Under the Sechelt Indian Self-Government Act (1986), the Sechelt community received title to their reserve lands. The Act enabled the Sechelt people to make their own constitution and decide on the form of government, membership code, legislative powers, and system of financial accountability. The elected council had powers to pass laws with regard to land and residence; administration and management of lands belonging to the band; education; social welfare and health services; and local taxation. However, some aboriginal groups criticized the Sechelt model as a municipal arrangement, governed by provincial legislation. According to them what the Sechelt band gained was only the right to manage some affairs, like municipalities.

It was no self-government in the true sense, for it did not challenge the provincial jurisdiction in any form.[28] Despite such criticism the Sechelt people felt that their unique model was necessitated by their particular needs and situation. The Act did not bar them from making further progress toward greater autonomy in the years to come.

Federal Initiatives for Empowerment of Indian Communities

After the Second World War the Indian Affairs Branch of the federal government underwent considerable changes. In 1949 the branch was transferred to the Department of Citizenship and Immigration. In 1962 the functions of the Indian Affairs Branch were regrouped under three major activities: education, operations, and support services. In 1966 the Department of Indian Affairs and Northern Development (DIAND) was established. Control and supervision of the Indian Affairs Branch, with associated powers and duties under the Indian Act, were transferred to DIAND from the Department of Citizenship and Immigration. Responding positively to NIB's policy paper, "Indian Control of Indian Education," the Canadian government began to emphasize local control of education, and started phasing churches out of Indian education and closing residential schools. After the Supreme Court's judgment in the Calder case in 1973 the federal government gradually gave up assimilatory policies and began exploring ways and means to accommodate aboriginal concerns and interests within the Canadian system. The Canadian government began taking definite measures to delegate more powers to the band governments, as well as recognizing the need for negotiated settlement with the Nisga'a and other Indian communities. It ensured that the Constitution Act of 1982 recognized and guaranteed aboriginal rights. Further, to conform with the equality rights clause in the Charter of Rights, the Indian Act was amended to remove the clause that had previously taken away Indian status from aboriginal women who married white men but granted such status to white women who married Indian men.

Bill C-32 passed by the House of Commons in 1985 reinstated treaty status to more than 22,000 men, women, and children and ensured access to federal programs and services for off-reserve Indians.[29] Responding to the recommendations of the Penner Committee, DIAND introduced Alternative Funding Arrangements (AFAs) in 1986. The federal government announced a new comprehensive claims policy without insisting on extinguishment of Indian rights and titles. It widened the scope of the comprehensive claims' negotiations by including issues like sharing of resource revenues and aboriginal people's participation in environmental decision making. The Kamloops Amendment to the Indian Act initiated in 1988 increased the powers of band councils to levy local taxes on Indian and non-native persons with interests on the reserve lands. The amendment allowed the bands to develop their lands through leases to non-Indian persons.[30] Aboriginal people now control over 80 percent of DIAND's program funding and aboriginal authorities increasingly deliver such services as education, language and culture, police services, health-care and social services, housing, property rights, and adoption and child welfare.[31]

Changes in British Columbia's Indian Policy

Provincial governments, unlike the federal government, were slow in responding to the natives' demand for recognition of their aboriginal rights. Taking the stand that constitutionally the responsibility of FNs lay with the federal government, for long the province of BC resisted the Canadian government's attempts to shift some of its responsibilities to the provinces.[32] Similarly, the province was reluctant to concede more powers to the band councils. However, after 1969 BC gradually accepted shouldering certain responsibilities like health, education, and social assistance especially for off-reserve Indians.[33] In 1975 the government of BC allowed the Nisga'a to have their own school district. A new district consisting of four villages was carved out wherein the Nisga'a were permitted to adopt their own curriculum, hire and fire the teachers, and control other aspects of education of their children. The health policy adopted in 1979 agreed in principle to delegate to the band councils the responsibility of providing health-care services to the native communities. In 1982 the province awarded a tree farm license to the Stuart-Trembleur band in northern BC. The provincial government also took the responsibility of providing services to non-status Indians. In 1982 the BC legislature passed Bill 58, the Indian Cut-Off Lands Disputes Act. The Act authorized the provincial government to enter into agreements with the Indian bands and federal government to resolve long-standing grievances over the loss of reserve lands in the early part of the century. In 1982 a royal commission of inquiry into Canada's fishing industry recommended that Indian claims on fish be acknowledged.[34]

Further, for more than a century the provincial political leadership in BC used the *terra nullius* argument to evade recognition of the existence of aboriginal rights. Governments and ruling parties at the provincial level always maintained that the aboriginal rights were extinguished long back with the colonization of their lands. Except for a few treaties initiated by Douglas prior to the emergence

of BC as a Crown colony,[35] no other treaties were concluded with the native communities. Compared to other
regions, the reserves in BC were smaller in size. In fact, in
order to accommodate the white settlers the provincial authorities took possession of a large chunk of land reserved
for FNs without any treaties. Once Indians became conscious of their rights and started organizing themselves they
began to claim aboriginal rights over the lands that were
taken over from them forcibly and without any treaties.
Apart from taking recourse to legal remedies, as was done
in legal cases like Calder, Guerin, Sparrow, and Delgamuukw, the FN communities in BC also resorted to road
blockades, rallies, hunger strikes, international pressure and
other forms of pressure to pressurize the governments to
accede to their demands.

The embarrassment created by the court rulings and
the problems created by the growing Indian activism forced
the Social Credit government headed by Bill Vander Zalm
to reconsider its policies toward the Indians. Acknowledging the political salience of Indian interests the government
created the Ministry of Native Affairs in 1989. During the
Oka Crisis of 1990 the FN communities in BC became
more militant and started taking direct action against logging, commercial fishing, and industrial ventures, causing
much anxiety to the governments as well as to business.
Premier Vander Zalm visited some of the blockades and
spoke with the protesters. The same year following a recommendation from his advisory council the premier announced that the province would enter into negotiations
with the Nisga'a. Even at that point of time BC was not
prepared to acknowledge the validity of aboriginal title.
The New Democratic Party (NDP), which took office
under Premier Mike Hartcourt in the 1990s also took active
interest in aboriginal affairs. The NDP expanded the role

and importance of the renamed Ministry of Aboriginal Affairs and recognized both aboriginal title and aboriginal right to self-government.[36]

The Royal Commission on Aboriginal Peoples

In the background of the Oka Crisis[37] and growing Indian militancy the federal government constituted a royal commission in 1991 to investigate and make recommendations on issues concerning the aboriginal peoples. The Royal Commission on Aboriginal Peoples (RCAP), comprising aboriginal and non-aboriginal representatives, completed its five-volume report in 1996. It called for a new relationship between aboriginal and non-aboriginal peoples based on recognition of the principles of equality, mutual respect, and reconciliation. To mitigate the effects of centuries of disasters and neglect the commission called for personal and collective healing for aboriginal peoples and communities. The commission emphasized mutually satisfactory negotiated agreements and endorsed the nation-to-nation paradigm as a way of conceptualizing the relationship between aboriginal nations and the Crown.[38] It recommended policies and programs that could break the cycle of poverty and dependency and ensure economic self-sufficiency for aboriginal peoples. Recognizing the aboriginal peoples' right to self-determination, the RCAP recommended formation of Indian self-governments within Canada to enable the Indian communities to take control of their collective future. The commission realized that Indian self-government would succeed only if the FN communities enjoyed a solid economic foundation and acquired developmental skills. To make the native governments self-reliant the commission called for a fair distribution of lands and resources and creation of their own sources of revenue

H. Srikanth

in the form of taxation, investment, borrowing, business fees and royalties, public corporation revenues, proceeds from lotteries and gaming, and so on. To support the rebuilding of aboriginal nations and to shift from paternalistic policies to partnership relations the commission made recommendations to the government for reaffirmation of Canada's respect for aboriginal peoples as distinct nations and admission of harmful actions by past governments.[39]

The report of the RCAP received wide publicity and considerable media attention. Many scholars and policy makers did not concur with the commission's contention that the aboriginal communities constituted distinct nations and that the future relationship between Canada and the First Nations should be based on a nation-to-nation relationship. Although the recommendations of the RCAP were viewed as too idealistic and impractical, they had some positive impact on the governments' Indian policy. In response to the commission's report the Government of Canada came out with an official document in 1998 entitled, "Gathering Strength – Canada's Aboriginal Action Plan." In the document the government admitted that:

> Our history with respect to the treatment of Aboriginal people is not something in which we can take pride. Attitudes of racial and cultural superiority led to a suppression of Aboriginal culture and values. As a country, we are burdened by past actions that resulted in weakening the identity of Aboriginal peoples, suppressing their languages and cultures, and outlawing spiritual practices. We must recognize the impact of these actions on the once self-sustaining nations that were disaggregated, disrupted, limited or even destroyed by the dis-

possession of traditional territory, by the relo-
cation of Aboriginal people, and by certain provisions of the Indian Act. We must
acknowledge that the result of these actions was
the erosion of the political, economic and social
systems of Aboriginal people and nations.[40]

Such an open admission of the mistakes of the past
did help in creating a congenial environment for reconciliation and cooperation between the FNs and the Canadian
government.

British Columbia Treaty Commission

The absence of federal treaties has been a major bone
of contention in BC. FNs in BC always argued that they had
been deprived of access to land and resources without their
consent and without any federal treaties. They confronted
the Canadian governments directly demanding protection of
aboriginal rights and their right to govern themselves. Uncertainties over land ownership of millions of acres of land led
to expensive legal battles, road or rail blockades, mobilization
of world opinion, and angry demonstrations. The Oka Crisis
in the 1990s and its repercussions in different parts of Canada
clearly indicated that if business companies and governments
continued to remain indifferent to aboriginal aspirations they
would have to pay a heavy price financially and politically.
During the Oka affair several FN communities in BC came
out openly in support of the Mohawks.
    Realizing the negative consequences of radicaliza-
tion of the aboriginal peoples' movement, both the federal
and BC governments began to take positive steps to move
away from the traditional Indian policy. Sensing a positive
change in the attitude of the governments, Bill Wilson,

chairperson of the First Nations Congress, organized two meetings of the First Nations, one with the premier of BC and the other with the prime minister of Canada. In these meetings, which took place in a cordial atmosphere, the parties acknowledged the need for cooperation and understanding. The governments consented to explore new means and mechanisms to address the First Nations' issues. Responding to the First Nations' proposal for a tripartite task force the British Columbia Claims Taskforce was created in December 1990 with seven members, two each from the federal and provincial governments and three from the First Nations Congress. The task force recommended the formation of a British Columbia Treaty Commission (in short, BCTC or BC Treaty Commission), comprising five members to oversee negotiations without becoming a party to them. It was suggested that any aboriginal community or combination of communities (e.g., tribal councils) could initiate negotiations. The negotiations would be broad enough to cover all important issues relating to territory, compensation, land management, resource development, protection of language and culture, taxation, and also self-government.[41]

The task force suggested a six-stage negotiation process involving all three parties – the Canadian government, the BC government, and the First Nations. In the first stage of the treaty negotiation process, the First Nations willing to negotiate would send "statements of intent" to the Treaty Commission indicating their intentions to negotiate treaties; in the second, the readiness of all three parties to enter treaty negotiations was to be assessed and established by the commission. Over the third, fourth, and fifth stages, the parties were to negotiate a framework agreement, an agreement-in-principle (AiP), and then a final agreement. When ratified by all three parties, the final agreement would become a treaty. In the sixth stage, the parties could also negotiate and agree to an openness proto-col to provide for citizen involvement through public ob-servation of negotiating sessions, media coverage, and public release of tabled documents.[42] Several First Nations which participated in the First Nations Summit supported the recommendations of the task force.

The NDP, which assumed office in 1992, went a step ahead of the Social Credit government by expanding the role of the newly renamed Ministry of Aboriginal Af-fairs and officially recognized both the aboriginal title and aboriginal right to self-government. In 1992 the two gov-ernments and the First Nations Summit signed the "British Columbia Treaty Commission Agreement," marking their formal acceptance of the task force's recommendation to start political negotiations to establish a new relationship based on mutual trust, respect, and understanding. The fed-eral and provincial governments agreed on a cost-sharing formula for treaty settlements: in general, the federal gov-ernment would provide cash, while the province would offer land. In 1993 the BC Treaty Commission was for-mally constituted and assigned with the responsibilities of facilitating the treaty process, disseminating information, raising public awareness, and providing loans to First Na-tions for starting treaty process–related activities.[43] The BCTC does not negotiate treaties; it only acts as the keeper of the treaty process in BC. The three parties at the negoti-ating tables are the First Nations, the Canadian govern-ment, and the government of BC. Behind these main parties are a host of third parties and related advisory structures which have an interest in treaty negotiations, often because of the legal rights, permits, or leases they hold.[44]

Modern Treaty Process in British Columbia: New Hopes and Old Problems

Immediately after the constitution of the BCTC the commission started receiving "statements of intent" from different First Nations. The actual negotiations began in 1994. According to an estimate, by October 1995, of the province's 198 FN communities, 130 of them (about 70 percent) had entered the treaty process.[45] While most communities are represented by the tribal councils some opted to negotiate individually. As of December 2006 there were 57 First Nations participating in the treaty process. Because some First Nations negotiate at a common table there were altogether 47 sets of negotiations.

At the time of writing this chapter (i.e. July 2008), six First Nations were in stage 2, four in stage 3, while stage 4 had 39 and stage 5 had eight. Maa-nulth First Nations, Lheidli T'enneh Band, Sliammon Indian Band, Tsawwassen First Nation, Yekooche Nation, and Yale First Nation signed AiPs, the blueprint for a final treaty. Lheidli T'enneh was foremost to ratify a treaty through the process. The Final Agreement provided Lheidli T'enneh First Nation a capital transfer of $13.2 million over 10 years, one-time funding of $12.1 million for implementation and transition costs, as well as $400,000 a year (indexed to inflation) for the next 50 years in resource revenue sharing. The land package included 4,330 hectares, a sizable portion within the city of Prince George.[46] It is anticipated that the conclusion of treaties would put an end to uncertainties and initiate economic development of the community and the region by ensuring adequate land, resources, and cash. The treaty commission claims that by putting an end to legal uncertainties, the treaties restore peace and understanding, attract private investment, and create more economic opportunities for the natives as well as non-natives.[47]

Many First Nations participating in the treaty process are going ahead with the negotiations with some expectations. But it needs to be stated here that not all First Nations of BC are optimistic about the treaty process. Approximately 30 percent of registered First Nations people in BC have not entered the treaty-making process. Leaders of some First Nations expressed no interest in the six-stage process of negotiations and are determined to assert aboriginal rights.[48] The UBCIC refused to participate in the treaty process on the ground that accepting the role of a provincial government in the negotiations would amount to acceptance of de facto displacement of aboriginal governments and their jurisdictions.[49] Many communities in the southern interior of the province, which are under the influence of UBCIC, did not respond positively to the treaty process for long.

Assessment of the Treaty Process

The treaty process, involving so many actors and interests, cannot but be quite complex. The process has to resolve many knotty issues. Although non-Indian communities are not involved directly in the negotiation process their concerns and interests cannot be totally ignored. Some critics felt that the government was yielding too much to the demands of the First Nations. According to one report the total financial cost of all treaties in BC is estimated to be $6.3–6.8 billion. The costs to be borne by the British Columbians (e.g., cash costs, pre-treaty and negotiation costs, provincial taxpayer's share of the federal government's costs) is expected to be $3.8–4.7 billion.[50] When the negotiation process was initiated it was assumed that tribal councils would represent different groups of First Nations in the treaty negotiation process. But fissures

H. SRIKANTH

and differences within councils led some individual First Nations to opt for direct negotiations. There are instances when First Nations whose members are not more than a couple of hundred have also opted to negotiate independently. Naturally, in such situations where more than the expected number of negotiating tables had to work, the negotiation process becomes overloaded and unable to deliver quick results.[51] The reluctance of the BC government to negotiate interim agreements also frustrated many a First Nation which expected quick results. Differences in perceptions of the Canadian government and the First Nations about the objectives of the treaty process also created tensions and misunderstanding between the two.

As such, the treaty process initiated in BC has many hurdles to cross. There have been moments of frustration, disappointment and anger for the parties. However, all three parties realize that there is no alternative. The failure of the treaty process only takes the situation back to the years of uncertainty and deadlock. The BC Treaty Commission takes every opportunity to remind the parties of the need for continuing with the negotiation process howsoever complex and time-consuming it might appear to be. The parties are advised to recognize the limits of one's own position and understand the expectations of others. It is held that with patience, firm commitment, courage, and creativity, it is possible to ensure successful negotiation and implementation of the treaties. The conclusion of an Umbrella Final Agreement (UFA) with the Council of Yukon Indians in 1993, the creation of a new territory of Nunavut for Inuit people in 1999, and the ratification of the Nisga'a Final Agreement Act in 2000 generate the hope that it is possible to reach agreements acceptable to all parties. The fact that by the end of 2006 eight First Nations had already signed AiPs and are ready for the Final Agreements also raises hopes about the possibility of successful negotiation of treaties under the BC treaty process. Since passing through all six stages does take considerable time, interim agreements may be concluded wherever possible so that the First Nations retain faith in the treaty process. The time taken for completion of the process may be reduced considerably if there are only a few negotiating tables. For that, First Nations should reconcile differences among themselves and come together as tribal groups. The first quarter of the twenty-first century will be the testing period for the treaty process.

Self-Government Experiments in Action

While continuing the treaty negotiations for settlement of their claims and demands, the First Nations have already started taking steps to give shape to self-governments of their choice. While most native communities accept the need for an elected leadership there are still many like Gitksan and Wet'suwet'en citizens who think that reverting to traditional systems of governance is necessary to realize self-government. There are some who look for a middle ground, wherein they can take advantage of the best of both worlds. In an interview one of the executive members of the Hupasceth First Nation told the author that their people wish to continue with the elected leadership, but at the same time they want to make use of the wisdom and experience of the traditional chiefs. Even in communities where there has been demand for handing over power to the traditional leadership it is accepted in principle that all decisions of the leadership have to be taken in public in consultation with all members of the First Nation. Similarly, Native women's organizations have made considerable inroads to make their viewpoints clear and have been pressurizing the Indian leaders to accommodate their inter-ests in the emerging political set-up. Several educated women are coming forward to take up executive and ad-ministrative positions in the Indian governments. Accord-ing to Phil Fontaine, FN National Chief, there are 109 First Nations' women chiefs while hundreds of women coun-cilors are leading the First Nations' people. About 20 per-cent of the First Nations' leaders today are women.[52]

It is true that incidences of corruption, wastage, and mismanagement of funds are visible here and there, as Flanagan and others have pointed out. It would, however, be premature at this moment to conclude that the First Na-tion governments have failed in all respects. If one evaluates the performance of FN governments from modern admin-istrative yardsticks one would probably jump only to neg-ative conclusions. Most Indian governments are inexperienced and lack professionalism, but if one evaluates their performance from the perspective of the needs of the FNs their achievements do not appear to be all that bad. Many have been trying to do justice to their communities by shouldering different responsibilities. Realizing the need for an adequate land base, all First Nations are pursuing the land claims. Having realized the price they have to pay for antagonizing the native communities different state agen-cies and private business enterprises working in the reserve areas have negotiated agreements with the First Nations, making them partners in business/development ventures. Some such enterprises like BC Hydro and Royal Bank have taken up initiatives for education, training, and employ-ment of FNs in their projects.[53]

Today, not all reserves are poor and underdevel-oped. Taking advantage of their location, physical re-sources, and social capital, some First Nations have initiated economic development programs that suit their interests and needs. Although own-source taxation still remains anathema to them many First Nations have begun exploring different alternative sources of income which would complement federal payments. By imposing taxes on non-aboriginal citizens, leasing reserve lands for commercial purposes, claiming royalties from non-aboriginal business enterprises operating on reserves, and entering into mutually-beneficial agreements with the corporate sector and state enterprises, the First Nations have been able to mobilize considerable resources for their governments. Gradually, many aboriginal Indians are entering business activities: approximately 20,000 aboriginal businesses are registered across Canada, about 4,700 of them in BC. FN enterprises are visible in the primary sector, manufacturing, and service sectors. Although most of them are small-scale enterprises catering to local markets, some even target international markets; 72 percent of aboriginal entrepreneurs reported profits in 2002; and 70 percent of aboriginal entrepreneurs residing in BC anticipated growth in the next two years as well. Making use of different tax concessions granted to them FN entrepreneurs are trying to create their own niche in the market in certain domains where they have advantages.[54]

One common identity marker that all First Nations use to distinguish themselves from the rapacious capitalist exploiters is that they pay respect to and live in harmony with nature and wildlife. Since they earn their livelihood basically from land, sea, and forest, they value the need for protecting biodiversity and advocate sustainable developmental strategies for development. The Canadian government and business enterprises operating in the reserve areas were, therefore, compelled to fall in line with the First Nations aspirations and reorient their development and business strategies in areas inhabited by aboriginal Indians. In collaboration with non-aboriginal business enterprises some First Nations have initiated development projects that suit their interests. For example, declaring their intention to conserve and use forests for increasing the incomes and economic opportunities for FNs, Nuu-chah-nulth First Nations of the central region founded Ma-Mook Natural Resources Ltd and signed an agreement with MacMillan Bloedel Ltd to form a joint forest venture company named Iisaak Natural Resources Ltd. The company is making efforts to develop and deliver innovative ways of managing the resources of Clayoquot Sound, respecting cultural, spiritual, recreational, economic, and scenic values. Through application of forest practices that respect ecological and cultural values, Iisaak is working toward environmentally sustainable forest initiatives that ensure protection and promotion of the interests of the First Nations.[55] The Osoyoos Indian Band Development Corporation, the economic development arm of the enterprising Osoyoos Indian Band, now manages 10 corporations operating in areas including tourism, recreation, agriculture, forestry, retail, and wine. Recently, Nk'Mip Cellars Winery started by the Osoyoos Indian Band Development Corporation entered into an agreement with Vincor International, based in Mississauga, Ontario to produce quality wine for export.[56] The Okanogan-based First Nations in BC are also making similar experiments.

Aboriginal tourism is another area where FNs are exploring opportunities for growth by keeping their environment and culture intact. Several enterprising First Nation citizens have started cultural centers, tourist resorts, adventure sports centers, and dance troupes. Nk'Mip Desert and Heritage Interpretive Centre started by Osoyoos Indian Band, Xa:ytem Longhouse Interpretive Centre located in Sto:lo traditional territory, K'san Interpretive

Village near Hazelton in Northern BC, Khowutzun Native Village in Duncan on Vancouver Island, Hiwus Feasthouse at the top of Grouse Mountain and Liliget Feast House in Vancouver, Takaya Tours operated by the Tsleil-Waututh Nation, and Le-la-la Dance Troupe from the Kwak waka'wakw Nation of Northern Vancouver Island are some of the FN initiatives in aboriginal tourism.

As such, hundreds of experiments in Indian self-government have been taking place on the reserves and in urban areas. Most of the initiatives mentioned above have been taken up only in recent decades, hence, not much is known about them. Except for studies by a few journalists like Dan Smith,[57] serious academic works or evaluative studies on functioning of these self-government experiments have not yet come out. Thus, it would be difficult to proclaim the success or failure of various native experiments in self-government at this point of time. Even as Alain Cairns admits:

At the moment, we have inadequate data on what works and what does not in either arena. I have asked various informed colleagues what percentage of existing First Nations governments are (*sic*) performing in excellent, adequate, or unacceptable ways. The responses are admittedly anecdotal, but the answers vary significantly. My conclusion is that we simply don't know.[58]

If the majority of the First Nations in BC succeed in concluding viable treaties and succeed in their experiments they would be able to show the way to First Nations in other provinces of Canada and also to the indigenous peoples elsewhere in the world. Only the future will tell whether the treaty negotiations and FN experiments with self-governments come out with something different and worthwhile to show to the world or whether they are only taking circuitous routes to finally get absorbed in the liberal capitalist framework of Canada.

Notes and References

1. The Indian Act differentiates between status and non-status Indians. Status Indians are those who are eligible to become band members and allowed to live on the reserves. The legal criteria as to who could be considered as status Indians are defined in the Indian Act itself. The Indians themselves had little choice to decide on who should be status or non-status members. See James S. Frideres, *Native People in Canada: Contemporary Conflicts* (Ontario: Prentice-Hall Canada, 1983), 20–32.
2. Allan D. McMillan and Eldern Yellowhorn, *First Peoples in Canada* (Vancouver: Douglas McIntyre, 2004), 129.
3. Frank Cassidy and Robert L. Bish, *Indian Government: Its Meaning in Practice* (Lantz Ville, BC: Oolichan Books and the Institute for Research on Public Policy, 1989), 46–9.
4. Sally W. Weaver, *Making Canadian Indian Policy: The Hidden Agenda 1968–70* (Toronto: University of Toronto Press, 1981), 18–19.
5.*First Nations in Canada* (Ottawa: Indian and Northern Affairs Canada, 2001).
6. Noel Dyck, *What is the Indian Problem?: Tutelage and Resistance in Canadian Indian Administration* (St Johns, Newfoundland: Institute of Social and Economic Research, 1991), 119–20.
7. Renee Dupuis, *Justice for Canada's Aboriginal Peoples* (Toronto: James Lorimer, 2002), 102–3.
8. H. B. Hawthorn and C. S. Belshow, *The Indians of British Columbia: A Study of Contemporary Social Adjustment* (Toronto: University of Toronto, 1958), 451.
9. Ibid., 458.

10. Except a few aboriginal communities covered under Treaty Eight concluded in 1899 in the northwest corner of BC, other parts of the province were not covered by federal treaties.

11. Frideres, *Native People*, 235-6.

12. Paul Tennant, "Native Indian Political Organization in British Columbia, 1900-1969: A Response to Internal Colonialism," *BC Studies* 55(1981): 26-49.

13. Paul Tennant, "Native Indian Political Activity in British Columbia, 1969-1983," *BC Studies* 57, Special Issue (Spring 1983): 112-14.

14. Rand Dyck, *Canadian Politics: Critical Perspectives* (Toronto: Nelson Canada, 2000), 73; also Weaver, *Making Canadian Indian Policy*, 20.

15. Rebecca Bateman, "Comparative Thoughts on the Politics of Accommodation," *BC Studies: The British Columbia Quarterly* 114 (Summer 1997): 68.

16. Augie Fleras and Jean Leonard Elliott, *Unequal Relations: An Introduction to Race and Ethnic Dynamics in Canada* (Toronto: Prentice Hall, 2002), 183.

17. Weaver, *Making Canadian Indian Policy*, 179.

18. Thomas R. Berger, "Native History, Native Claims and Self-Determination," *BC Studies* Special Issue, 57(Spring 1983): 17-18.

19. Tennant, "Native Indian Political Activity, 120-2.

20. Robert J. Muckle, *The First Nations of British Columbia: An Archaeological Survey* (Vancouver: UBC Press, 1988), 73.

21. Wotherspoon Satzewich, *First Nations: Race, Class and Gender Relations* (Scarborough: Nelson Canada, 1993), 233-4.

22. Quebec is a Francophone-dominant province in Canada. There has been a strong movement for greater autonomy for Quebec within Canada. Radical nationalists among the Quebec Francophones have been demanding secession of Quebec from Canada. In recent years Canada has been using the ideology of multiculturalism to corner the Quebec separatists. Refer Francois Rocher and Miriam Smith, *New Trends in Canadian Federalism* (Toronto: Broadway Press, 2003), 85-106.

23. Muckle, *The First Nations of British Columbia: An Archaeological Survey*.

24. From *Public Policy and Aboriginal Peoples 1965-1992*, vol. 2 (Ottawa: RCAP, 1994), 78-9.

25. Anthony J. Long and Menno Boldt, eds., *Governments in Conflict? Provinces and Indian Nations in Canada* (Toronto: University of Toronto Press, 1988), 39–41.

26. Anthony J. Long, Leroy Little Bear and Menno Boldt, eds., *Pathways to Self-Determination: Canadian Indians and the Canadian State* (Toronto: University Of Toronto Press, 1984), 77.

27. Dyck, *Indian Problem*, 149.

28. Jill Wherrett, *Aboriginal Self-Government* (Ottawa: Library of Parliament, 1996), 12.

29. Dyck, *Canadian Politics*, 74; Shirley Joseph, "Assimilation Tools: Then and Now," *BC Studies* 89 (Spring 1991): 69.

30. Wherrett, *Aboriginal Self-Government*, 10.

31. Dyck, *Canadian Politics*, 77.

32. Long and Boldt, *Governments in Conflict*, 45–7.

33. Robert Exell, "History of Indian Claims in B.C.," *Advocate* 48:6 (December 1990): 866–880. .

34. Berger, "Native History, 20–1.

35. During his tenure as governor of Vancouver Island, James Douglas negotiated 14 agreements with the FN communities and acquired land measuring 358 sq m. Douglas could not go ahead with such treaties due to paucity of funds. For more details about Douglas' Indian policy, see Paul Tennant, *Aboriginal Peoples and Politics: The Indian Land Question in British Columbia 1849–1989* (Vancouver: UBC Press, 1989), 26–38; also Robin Fisher, *Contact and Conflicts: Indian-European Relations in British Columbia, 1774–1890* (Vancouver: UBC Press, 1992), 49–72.

36. Paul Tennant, "Aboriginal Peoples and Aboriginal Title in British Columbia Politics," in *Politics, Policy and Government in British Columbia*, ed. R. K. Carty (Vancouver: UBC Press, 1996), 55–56, 62.

37. In 1990 the Mohawks set up a road blockade for 78 days to prevent the nearby town of Oka from expanding a golf course onto land the Mohawks considered their own. The agitation turned violent and a police officer was killed. The government had to mobilize the Canadian armed forces to remove the blockade.

38. Frances Abele and Michael J. Prince, "Aboriginal Governance and Canadian Federalism: A To-Do List for Canada," in *New Trends in Canadian Federalism*, ed. Francois Rocher and Miriam Smith (Toronto: Broadway Press, 2003), 141.

39. *People to People, Nation to Nation: Highlights from the Report of the Royal Commission on Aboriginal People* (Ottawa: Library and Archives Canada, 1996), 26-7.

40.Ministry of Indian Affairs and Northern Development, *Gathering Strength: Canada's Aboriginal Action Plan* (Ottawa: DIAND, 1997), 4.

41. Tennant, "Aboriginal Peoples," 58-9.

42. Abele and Prince, "Aboriginal Governance," 149.

43. Tennant, "Aboriginal Peoples," 63.

44. Abele and Prince, "Aboriginal Governance," 147-8.

45. Tennant, "Aboriginal Peoples," 63.

46. "Negotiations Update: December 2006," BC Treaty Commission, http://www.bctreaty.net/files/updates.php accessed 16 April 2007.

47. "Why Treaties? A Legal Perspective," BC Treaty Commission, http://www.bctreaty.net/files/pdf_documents/why_treaties.pdf accessed 4 September 2007; also "Treaties are Good for the Economy," BC Treaty Commission, http://www.bctreaty.net/files/economic-ed1.php accessed 16 April 2007.

48. Muckle, *First Nations*, 85.

49. Tennant, "Aboriginal Peoples," 62.

50. Christopher McKee, *Treaty Talks in British Columbia* (Vancouver: UBC Press, 2000), 108.

51. "Looking Back, Looking Forward: A Review of the BC Treaty Process," BC Treaty Commission, http://www.bctreaty.net/files_2/pdf_documents/review_bc_treaty_process.pdf accessed 16 April 2007.

52. See Phil Fontaine's address to the First Nations Women Leaders Forum, Vancouver, BC (February 2007), http://www.turtleisland.org/discussion/viewtopic.php?p=7997&sid=c94cc136f052e280bc19ab5fa4107c74 accessed 14 December 2007.

53. See "Initiatives," BC Hydro, http://www.bchydro.com/ard/initiatives/initiatives905.html accessed 14 December 2007; "RBC Aboriginal Student Awards Program," Royal Bank of Canada (12 May 2005), http://www.rbc.com/uniquecareers/campus/aboriginal-student-awards.html accessed 14 December 2007.

54. "Aboriginal Entrepreneurs Survey 2002," *Daily* (27 September 2004), http://www.statcan.ca/Daily/English/040927/d040927d.htm accessed 14 December 2007; Aboriginal Business Service Network, "BC Aboriginal Entrepreneurs: A Growing Force: BC Aboriginal Small Business Profile," http://www.firstbusiness.ca/guides/bc_aes_profile.pdf accessed 14 December 2007.
55. See "Approach," Iisaak Forest Resources (2000), http://www.iisaak.com/approach.html accessed 14 December 2007.
56. "Major Aboriginal Businesses Launched in British Columbia's South Okanagan Region," Indian and Northern Affairs Canada, http://www.ainc-inac.gc.ca/nr/prs/s-d2002/index_e.html accessed 25 February 2008.
57. Dan Smith, *The Seventh Fire: The Struggle for Aboriginal Government* (Toronto: Key Porter Books, 1993).
58. Cairns and Flanagan, "An Exchange," 114.

H. Srikanth

5

LIMITS OF POLITICAL AUTONOMY AND PROBLEMS OF DEVELOPMENT IN HILL AREAS

The persistent struggles of the FNs and the relentless campaigns of scholars and activists have succeeded in compelling the Canadian state to acknowledge the rights of indigenous communities and take initiatives for reconciliation and revitalization of the relations between Canada and the indigenous peoples. Efforts are underway to give shape to new economic and political arrangements acceptable to all three parties: the federal government, the provincial government, and the First Nations. On their part, the FN communities have started exploring appropriate forms of self-government. It is still not clear as to what the future of native self-governments would be. Only after a decade or so would it be possible to assess how far the new arrangements are better compared to political regimes under DIAND and how far they succeed in upholding the interests of the FN communities.

Unlike in Canada, the tribal communities in India, especially the hill tribes of northeast India, have experimented with different political arrangements conceived to satisfy the desire of tribals for autonomy. In addition to the special rights guaranteed to all tribal communities, new constitutional arrangements and political institutions, absent in other parts of India, were conceived and implemented in the hill areas of composite Assam. To accommodate the growing political aspirations of the hill tribes the political map of composite Assam was changed drastically giving birth to new states. Centering around the working of the political institutions conceived by the Indian constitution this chapter examines the political developments that have taken place after the 1950s in response to the political aspirations and movements of the indigenous communities for greater autonomy. In the background of intellectual debates taking place on issues of tribal autonomy and development, the chapter explores the efficacy of the new political initiatives and developmental strategies in ensuring the autonomy and progress of the hill communities in the erstwhile composite Assam.

Tribal Communities under Post-Colonial Rule

On the eve of independence, the Indian nationalist leaders realized the need to undo colonial policies and address the problems of integrating the tribal communities into the national mainstream. During this period, two dominant lines of thought took shape on the question of tribal development. One argued that the tribal peoples were actually backward Hindus, hence the British attempts at differentiating tribal peoples from other backward communities was a colonial conspiracy to divide the Indians. This line of thought appealed for putting an end to the isolationist policies pursued by British administrators and anthropologists. It argued that tribal people could progress only through assimilation into the cultural and economic mainstream of the Indian nation. In the context of northeast India this point of view has been strongly advocated by G. S. Ghurye.[1] In contrast, Verrier Elvin, who played a very important role in shaping the country's tribal policy during the Nehruvian era, believed in the need to allow consider-

H. Srikanth

able autonomy to the tribal people, enabling them to manage their own affairs. Although many nationalist Indians branded him an isolationist who wished to keep the tribal people only as museum pieces, Elvin made it clear in several of his later writings that he was all for the development of tribal peoples; he stood for a particular pattern of development that would preserve and promote all that was good and worth preserving among the tribal people.[2] Much of his ideas found official support and political expression in the form of Nehru's policy of Panchsheel for tribal development.[3] This political and intellectual debate between assimilationists and autonomists has considerably influenced the constitutional provisions and government policies in post-colonial India.

Taking note of the plight of tribal people in the country, the Constitution of India has incorporated several provisions for protecting and promoting their interests.[4] The Fundamental Rights guaranteed in the constitution ensured that the tribal people are treated as equal to other citizens and that they are not discriminated in matters of public employment and accessibility to public resources. Practices such as forced labor and *begar* have been declared unconstitutional. The rights guaranteed to the minorities ensured the tribes of their right to protect their culture, religion and language. While guaranteeing equality of opportunity for all citizens, Clauses 4 and 4(A) of Article 16 made it clear that the state can make provision for reservations in services for backward communities not represented in government services. According to Article 46 of Part IV (Directive Principles of the State Policy) of the Constitution:

The state shall promote with special care the educational and economic interests of the weaker sections of the people and in particular of the scheduled castes and the scheduled tribes, and shall protect them from social injustice and all forms of exploitation.

Apart from guaranteeing Fundamental Rights, the Indian Constitution made special provisions for the benefit of Scheduled Castes (SCs) and Scheduled Tribes (STs)[5] to ensure fair representation for them in education, employment, and in sharing of political power. Articles 330 and 332 made provision for reservation of seats for SCs and STs in Parliament and the state legislatures; Article 243-D ensured reservation of seats for them in panchayats. Apart from these constitutional provisions for reservations, the constitution has included certain provisions keeping in view the specific requirements of STs alone. It empowers the President of India to designate tribal-dominant areas and scheduled areas and ensure autonomy and protection to tribal people through appropriate mechanisms. The constitution incorporates the Fifth and Sixth Schedules specifying special provisions, privileges, immunities and powers that the STs living in scheduled areas are entitled to (Articles 244 and 244A). These schedules deal elaborately with the functions, duties, and responsibilities of the governments and functionaries at different levels in the scheduled areas. The state governors are given powers to stop implementation of laws and policies that could have adverse effects on tribal people in the scheduled areas and make appropriate recommendations to the governments for tribal development. Article 275 promises grants-in-aid to be made available from the Consolidated Fund of India each year for promoting the welfare of the STs and for administration of scheduled areas. The recurring and non-recurring expenditure for the development of scheduled areas and for STs has also been charged from the Consolidated Fund of India.

In pursuit of the constitutional goals, 7.5 percent of seats in government-aided educational institutions and the same percentage of jobs in government and public sector undertakings are earmarked for STs. Forty-one out of 543 Parliament seats and 530 out of a total of 4,072 legislative assembly seats are allocated for STs. Although these reservations were initially meant for only 10 years, the constitution is amended from time to time to ensure that the reservation policy continues. Following the 73rd Amendment of the Constitution, a certain number of seats and positions are reserved for STs even in the grass-roots Panchayati Raj institutions.[6]

The rights guaranteed to minorities enabled the STs to secure immunity from the Hindu Civil Code and allowed them to practice their customary laws with respect to marriage, inheritance, adoption, divorce, and so forth. After independence, several commissions were appointed to understand the problems of tribal communities and make appropriate recommendations for their development. All Five Year Plans made allocations for tribal development under different heads. In the 1970s the central government introduced the Tribal Sub-Plan (TSP) strategy in the planning process, earmarking a portion of funds for development of tribal pockets in the states where tribal people are still minorities. The central government has been insisting upon all its departments to assign 8 percent of their allocation for tribal needs. In proportion to the tribal population, the state governments are also asked to set aside a part of their budget for tribal welfare. The government has sought to encourage education among tribal people at all levels through residential schools, vocational training centers, hostels, scholarships, and fellowships. Different organizations like the Tribal Co-operative Marketing Development Federation of India Ltd (TRIFED), National Scheduled

Tribes Finance and Development Corporation (NSTFDC), National Commission of Scheduled Tribes, and others have been created to look into the various economic and social needs of the STs.[7] At the center, a separate Ministry of Tribal Affairs was created in 1999 to plan and coordinate different programs for the development of the STs. Some state governments have also created ministries exclusively for tribal welfare and development. Several schemes and programs have been and are being launched and implemented both by the central and different state governments for tribal development.

Political and Constitutional Changes in Northeast India

Apart from these general political and constitutional developments that influence all tribal communities in the country, the Constitution of India made special provisions for the tribal communities inhabiting the hill areas of composite Assam. As discussed in Chapter 3, during the colonial period the British followed the policy of least interference in the internal affairs of the hill communities. The Inner Line Regulations were invoked to restrict the entry of people from the plains into the hill areas. By declaring them scheduled districts or backward areas the British ensured that the hill administration was kept outside the purview of the laws and institutions that governed other areas of British India. Although some hill areas like the Khasi-Jaintia Hills, Mikir, North Cachar Hills, Naga, and Lushai Hills were brought under some kind of administration under the supervision of political agents or political officers, the North-Eastern Frontier Tracts bordering Tibet and Myanmar were left almost unadministered. Tribal chiefs loyal to the British received colonial patron-

H. SRIKANTH

age. Where the tribal chiefs were found unreliable, the British created new positions from among the natives. Even in such areas the authorities retained many of the tribal institutions and practices and initiated only marginal changes in their structures and functions to suit their colonial interests. In spite of all these, some changes did take place in the lives of the hill peoples during the British regime. The spread of Christianity and the development of modern education in the hills created indigenous educated middle classes. In the Lushai Hills the upcoming English-educated middle classes led by the Mizo Union opposed the oppressive Mizo chiefs and demanded abolition of chieftainships. Such a radical demand to do away with the traditional political institution was absent among the Nagas where the traditional chiefs appear to be comparatively more democratic and less authoritarian. Among the Khasis, the ascendancy of pro-Indian educated middle classes over the traditional chiefs was gradual and peaceful. The traditional chiefs in the Naga Hills continued to retain considerable hold over the people, despite the emergence of new social forces from within. However, in the North-Eastern Frontier Tracts, which were declared as excluded areas and almost left unadministered, traditional tribal institutions worked unhindered during the British regime.

When India gained independence it inherited the hill areas with all their colonial baggage. Although the Indian nationalist movement had little influence on the hill communities the Indian elite which took over political power from the British were averse to giving up control over the hill areas of northeast India. The Indian leadership aspired to bring the hill communities into the national mainstream by putting an end to the colonial policy of keeping the hill tribes aloof from the rest of India. But at the same time the leaders also realized the need for addressing the fears and concerns of the hill communities by granting them considerable autonomy in their internal affairs. Accordingly, the Constitution of India made provision for the Sixth Schedule which intended to create Autonomous District Councils (ADCs) in the Naga, Lushai, Khasi-Jaintia, Mikir, and North Cachar Hills.

The district and regional councils under the Sixth Schedule areas were entrusted with the responsibility of taking appropriate measures to protect the land, resources, culture, language, and identity of the tribal communities inhabiting the hills. However, keeping in view the strategic consideration and communication bottlenecks the North-Eastern Frontier Tracts were kept outside the purview of the Sixth Schedule. The Naga leadership in the Naga Hills District, which had strong reservations against joining the Indian Union, rejected the autonomous district status and took to arms to fight for independence. But other designated hill communities accepted the new institutional arrangements conceived in the Sixth Schedule. The ADCs and regional councils constituted through democratic elections played a significant role in imparting training to the tribal people in the art of governance within the liberal constitutional framework. The ADCs formulated their own laws relating to the terms of office, transfer of land, land revenue, trade by non-tribals, administration of justice, appointment and succession of traditional chiefs, taxation, and audits.[8] Compared to the tribal areas included in the Fifth Schedule of the Indian Constitution the Sixth Schedule areas enjoyed more powers. Yet, the working of the district councils under the Sixth Schedule attracted considerable criticism from scholars and activists.

Performance of Autonomous District Councils

Scholars like V. Venkat Rao, L. S. Gassah and R. N. Prasad, who studied the working of district councils under the Sixth Schedule areas have pointed out several limitations in the working of ADCs.[9] Legally speaking, the district councils enjoy some amount of autonomy, but in practice they are not immune to external influences. The state governments control and influence the working of district councils in different ways. The state governors often use their power of nominations to tilt majorities in ADCs to suit the interests of governments in power at the state levels. The party or parties in power at the state level indirectly influence the district council politics. Competitive party politics and political defections, unknown to the traditional tribal societies, adversely affect the functioning of the district councils. It is also alleged that the state governments usually delay the transfer of funds assigned under Article 275 of the Constitution to the district councils and at times avoid paying royalties that are due to them. Inadequacy of funds forces the district councils to adopt undesirable practices like felling of timber beyond ecologically sound management limits and large-scale leasing out of community lands to private persons.[10]

In addition to external influences the district councils suffer from internal limitations as well. It has been observed that the leadership at the district level does not exhibit the required political acumen and vision. It lacks creativity and expertise in planning and policy making and does not take full advantage of the powers and resources assigned or available to it. Although they have been given constitutional and legal rights the district councils often hesitate to impose taxes and mobilize internal resources.[11] Quite often even the funds available to them are not utilized or properly utilized. Many scholars who studied the functioning of different district councils pointed out financial irregularities, mismanagement and lack of accountability. Political patronage, nepotism and favoritism influence the recruitment of staff responsible for policy making. Most teachers recruited in the educational institutions run by the district councils are less qualified and underpaid. Although they had powers to constitute courts, some district councils avoided having their own courts due to inadequacy of funds. Even where they were constituted, the standard of persons put in charge of those courts was found to be very low. Naturally, the value of services offered by them remained poor.[12]

Critics have also pointed out that the district councils are often dominated by dominant indigenous tribes. Ethnic minorities rarely find representation in the councils. Some Autonomous Regional Councils (ARCs) allege that the district councils do not share royalties with them and that they do not permit teaching at the primary-school level in local tribal languages. Naturally, the unrepresented or underrepresented ethnic minorities, as in Mizoram, come in conflict with dominant tribes and make demands for the creation of separate district councils for them.[13] It is held that the new political leadership, instead of utilizing the services of the traditional political institutions, treats them as competitors and makes utmost efforts to marginalize or subordinate them to the constitutional machinery.[14]

Deficiencies in the working of district and regional councils led to a search for alternatives. Regular audit of finances by the Comptroller and Auditor General of India, appointment of the State Finance Commission for authorizing funds, direct funding by the central government, effective mobilization of internal sources for increasing finances, delegating more powers and control over resources, appli-

H. SRIKANTH

cation of anti-defection laws, ensuring representation and involvement of women, minorities and of NGOs in policy formulation and program implementation are some important proposals made for improving the effective functioning of the ADCs. The governments took note of some such expert suggestions and initiated some reforms. But those measures do not seem to have led to any qualitative change in the structure and functioning of the district and regional councils.

From District Councils to Separate States

In the 1950s when hill districts were still part of composite Assam different tribal leaders in the hills accused the state government for the failure of ADCs in accomplishing the tasks for which they were constituted. They complained of limited powers and resources of the district councils. After experimenting with ADCs for about a decade, dominant hill communities such as the Khasis, Jaintias, Garos, and Mizos inhabiting composite Assam began to agitate for tribal-dominant states. Their movements yielded results with the formation of the tribal-dominant states of Meghalaya in 1972 and Mizoram in 1986.[15] While the Khasis, Jaintias, and Garos achieved the state of Meghalaya through a peaceful movement, the Mizos went through a violent insurgent movement before they could achieve state status. The formation of tribal-dominant states did bring some changes in the structure and functioning of district and regional councils already working in the hill areas. The inclusion of Clause 12A in the Sixth Schedule has enabled the state government to undermine the powers of the district councils in Meghalaya.[16] After the formation of Mizoram, the Mizo District Council was abolished and the regional councils operating in the areas inhabited by other tribal ethnic minorities were upgraded to district councils. However, as in Meghalaya, the state government in Mizoram has acquired overriding powers over the district councils in the state. As such, tensions between the district councils and the state governments continued even after the formation of tribal-dominant states.

At the time when the hill communities in the Khasi-Jaintia Hills and Mizo Hills were fighting for separate states for tribals the two other hill districts of composite Assam, namely, the North Cachar Hills and Mikir Hills (now Karbi-Anglong) accepted the guarantees given by the Government of Assam and chose to remain in the state of Assam. However, in the 1980s and 1990s these hill areas witnessed a mass movement for creation of an autonomous state.[17] Of late, some militant outfits among the Karbis and Dimasas are raising demands for separate states and taking to terrorist means to achieve their goals. In recent years, militant groups have appeared even in Meghalaya demanding separate states for the Garos and Khasi-Pnars. Their militant activities have not yielded any results yet. At the moment the Government of India is reluctant to accede to any further demands for reorganization of the northeastern region. However, the government does not seem to be averse to conceding the demands for creation of more district or regional councils and to grant of greater autonomy to the units under the Sixth Schedule as long as such demands do not disturb the boundaries of the existing states in any way.

H. SRIKANTH

Political Developments in Non-Scheduled Hill Areas of Composite Assam

The ADCs, in a way, paved the way for the formation of the new tribal-dominant states of Meghalaya and
Mizoram. But the Naga Hills District and the North-Eastern Frontier Tracts also attained state status although they
did not experiment with the ADC system at all. As early as
in 1963, realizing the futility of using the Armed Forces to
deal with the defiant Naga tribes, Jawaharlal Nehru sought
to appease their quest for autonomy by creating a new state
of Nagaland by uniting the Naga Hills District and the
Tuensang area of NEFA. The Indian Constitution was
amended to guarantee to the Nagas that no Act or law
passed by the Union Parliament affecting the Naga religious
or social practices, their customary law and procedures,
civil and criminal justice, and the ownership and transfer
of land and resources, shall have any legal force in Nagaland
unless accepted by a majority vote in the Nagaland Legislative Assembly.[18] The new state was initially placed under
the Ministry of External Affairs and was given a wide range
of immunities. Traditional tribal political institutions continued to operate at the grass roots and the state government chose not to do anything drastic that would
undermine the authority of the tribal leaders. The traditional tribal councils were allowed to have control over
their villages as per the Chin Hills Regulation Act of 1896.
The state government operates in the Naga villages through
the village councils wherein the tribal elders continue to
enjoy legitimacy and respect.

Political developments in the North-Eastern Frontier Tracts took a different path. In 1954 the hill areas of
the North-Eastern Frontier Tracts were reconstituted and
brought together as the North-East Frontier Agency

(NEFA). However, after the defeat of India in the Sino-Indian War of 1962 the Indian administration began to intervene actively in the region for strategic reasons. In 1972 NEFA was given Union Territory status and renamed Arunachal Pradesh. The first elected legislative assembly came into existence in 1978. In 1986 Arunachal Pradesh became a separate state within the Indian Union. The Panchayati Raj institutions which were experimented with in other parts of India were introduced in NEFA in 1967 with some modifications. After the Constitution Act (73rd Amendment) in 1992, and then with the passing of the Arunachal Pradesh Panchayati Raj Act, 1997, the earlier system was replaced by a three-tier Panchayati Raj system as exists in other parts of the country. With the penetration of parliamentary institutions the significance of traditional tribal institutions has declined considerably in general. Yet, among certain communities traditional political institutions continue to play some role in matters relating to settlement of disputes and administration of justice at the community level. The Khonoma and other grass-roots experiments in Nagaland show that traditional institutions need not necessarily be barriers to implementation of new and innovative schemes for development.[19]

Debate on Empowerment of Tribal Communities and Traditional Institutions

Conceding more powers to the district councils in North Cachar and Karbi-Anglong and creation of tribal-dominant states of Meghalaya, Mizoram, and Arunachal Pradesh were viewed by many as empowerment of the hill tribes. However, scholars like B. K. Roy Burman and B. D. Sharma opined that all these developments only strengthened the formal system of governance by the state structures. According to them the real contradiction in the tribal areas is between the community and the structures of the State. In place of community-led governance the post-colonial state has introduced a formal system of self-governance which allows little space for the autonomous and creative role of the communities and alienates the tribal people from their natural settings. As the State structures and market forces acquire more authority, the communities get weakened. These critics feel that unlike traditional governance, which had its roots in the culture and history of the people, the new constitutional arrangements enjoy little legitimacy among the hill tribes, not having liberal traditions. The tribal people, who believe in the communitarian principle of consensus, could not identify themselves with the new political institutions based on the values of individualism and competition.

The formal system of governance experimented with in the region has further weakened the authority of the traditional political institutions and undermined the customary rights of the communities over their own resources and destinies.[20] The growing civil unrest, political instability, corruption, and inefficiency of the governments in the hill states are often attributed to the decline of traditional political institutions. The only way out of the impasse would then be through the restoration of the traditional authority of the community.[21] Partly, these ideas found legal expression with the enactment of the Panchayats Extension to Scheduled Areas (PESA) Act of 1996. Activists like B. D. Sharma who were instrumental in drafting PESA are now actively campaigning for extension of PESA to the Sixth Schedule areas of northeast India.

Despite such faith reposed in the traditional institutions by some, one should avoid making sweeping generalizations about the traditional tribal institutions' abilities to empower the hill communities. That the tribal communities and traditional institutions need not always be complementary becomes clear from the fact that the Mizo people themselves have rejected the traditional chieftainship as they felt that their tribal chiefs were not really representing the interests of the communities. Even in the North Cachar Hills and Karbi-Anglong, where the powers of the traditional chiefs have been taken away, there has not been any popular resentment against the state move. Yet, it needs to be admitted that among certain tribal communities traditional political institutions and tribal chiefs do enjoy a degree of legitimacy. Although they may not have constitutional recognition some of the traditional institutions like *dorbars* in Meghalaya, village councils in Nagaland, and *kebang* in Arunachal Pradesh do play significant roles at the grass roots level, providing services and security to their communities in areas under their control.

In Meghalaya, as David Syiemlieh pointed out, even arms of the government such as district councils, police and the municipality depend on *dorbars* for a variety of purposes like issue of residence certificates to individuals, implementation of health and sanitation programs, processing of applications for licenses, ensuring support to the local police for maintenance of peace and order, and so forth. Because of the legitimacy and respect that they command it is often argued that *dorbars* can function better than the bureaucratically-administered institutions.[22] In view of the advantages that traditional institutions have, scholars like Bengst Karlsson supported the idea for constitutional recognition of traditional institutions, as demanded by the Khasi *syiems*.[23] The Working Paper prepared by the National Commission for Review of the Indian Constitution in 2001 has also formally supported the idea of constitutional recognition and direct funding for the traditional institutions that are still functional in states like Meghalaya.[24]

It, however, needs to be stated that the suggestions for constitutional recognition of traditional institutions were not supported by all. Critics like Apurba K. Baruah, Rajesh Dev and Manorama Sharma pointed out that even in states where there has been such a demand, everything is not right with the traditional institutions. They cite contradictions between liberal democratic values enshrined in the Indian Constitution and the "communitarian" perspectives propounded by indigenous scholars and activists.[25] According to them the *dorbars* are undemocratic since they are dominated by particular clans and have no representation for women.[26] Interpreting the colonial history of the Khasi community Manorama Sharma argues that what is often projected as tradition is not in fact very old as it is presumed to be and that much of what has been viewed as tradition has its origins only in the colonial period.[27]

Baruah contends that more than anyone else it is the upwardly mobile new indigenous elite that have been talking about tradition with the clear-cut idea of protecting and promoting their own class interests. Although the traditional institutions have some relevance in village areas inhabited by people belonging to the same tribe, they become anachronistic in urban areas peopled by different tribes and non-tribals. Non-representation of people from other communities makes the traditional institutions appear anachronistic. Analyzing the processes at work in Laitumukhrah *Dorbar* in the city of Shillong, Baruah notes that it is not tradition per se that commands respect in Laitumukhrah: it is the power derived partly from the ethnically mobilized community, and partly from acting as an arm of the state with its apparatuses of coercion and patronage that result in the de facto legitimacy of the institution of *dorbar*.[28] Hence, these scholars suggest that before the governments accede to the demand for constitutional recognition of institutions like *dorbars* and *himas* the state should exert pressure on the communities to democratize the traditional institutions to ensure participation of women and ethnic minorities. Such demands for more participative and gender-sensitive traditional institutions have been echoed even by indigenous scholars like Toki Blah and David Syiemlieh.[29]

Economic Foundations for Tribal Autonomy

Appropriate political institutions and arrangements are no doubt essential conditions for tribal self-government. But no political arrangements can sustain themselves without a strong and viable economic base. During the pre-colonial period the tribal communities had access to land, forests, and other resources essential for their survival. With shifting cultivation (*jhum*), supplemented by food-gathering, hunting, and trade with people in the plains the hill tribes were able to sustain themselves. In times of extreme scarcity the hill tribes would attack and plunder the villages in the plains. Their traditional sociopolitical institutions then reflected both the needs and limitations of the tribal economic base.

But what happens when the political institutions and economic base of a given community are in conflict with each other? Can traditional political institutions survive if their economic base has changed considerably? To look at it the other way, will the modern constitutional mechanisms work if the tribal economic base remains unchanged? To seek answers for such questions, one needs to undertake the strenuous task of examining the working of political institutions of tribal communities in light of changes taking place in the tribal economy since the colonial period. Of course, there are quite a few studies in India that have thrown light on the impact of colonial and post-colonial economies on tribal communities. In the context of northeast India, some scholars have made references to the origins and growth of educated middle classes within the tribal communities and their impact on ethnic movements in the region. But how the changing economy and the resulting class differences within the hill communities affect the traditional tribal economy and in what ways these changes influence the structure and functioning of the existing tribal self-governments need to be examined in greater detail. Keeping these aspects in mind, one may examine three vital and interdependent components of traditional tribal economy: shifting cultivation, dependence on forests, and control over community resources.

Shifting Cultivation

Unlike the indigenous peoples in British Columbia who depended mostly on fishing and hunting for their livelihood, agriculture continues to be the main source of livelihood for the hill tribes in northeast India since time immemorial. Except certain tribal communities like the Angamis and Chakasang which are familiar with settled and terrace cultivation, most tribal communities in the hills practice shifting cultivation. This type of farming is also known as slash-and-burn cultivation, or *podu* or *jhum* cultivation. Estimates of the number of families dependent on, and the number of hectares of land under, shifting cultivation vary considerably.

Table 5.1 shows that the minimum area under shifting cultivation at one time or another in Assam, Arunachal Pradesh, Mizoram, Nagaland, and Meghalaya put together is 9,945 sq km. The annual area under shifting cultivation is around 2,656 sq km. The total number of families depending on shifting cultivation in these states is 350,336.[30]

Many scholars and officials view shifting cultivation as primitive vandalism that causes permanent and cumulative degradation of the quality of the environment and adds to deforestation, destruction of bio-diversity, soil erosion, and a consequent drop in rainfall. However, some scholars contend that shifting cultivation does not pose much of a problem as long as the population is limited and *jhuming* cycles are long. But with the rapid growth of population and consequent reduction of the cycle of shifting cultivation from 20 years to about five years, scholars contend that shifting cultivation has become a potential threat to the environment.[31] The intellectuals who subscribe to this view have recommended that the Indian government take appropriate steps to discourage shifting cultivation, provide incentives to the *jhumis* to switch over to settled cultivation, take up afforestation programs, rehabilitate the shifting cultivators, and show them alternative sources of income by encouraging them to take to horticulture, floriculture, pisciculture, and cultivation of commercially viable species like rubber, and medicinal plants.[32] Responding positively to such suggestions and recommendations, both the central and state governments in the northeastern states have taken up programs to contain shifting cultivation by encouraging settled cultivation and afforestation programs in the hill areas.

As against the dominant perception of shifting cultivation discussed above, there are scholars and activists who believe that the practice of shifting cultivation in the hills has its own logic. In his book, *A Philosophy for NEFA*, Verrier Elwin cautioned that one should be careful in taking steps against shifting cultivation, as the practice is indispensable to tribal culture, tradition, religion and identity.[33] Supporting Elvin's contention, some scholars came out with arguments that shifting cultivation is not as dangerous as it is projected to be. Daman Singh, who placed the average loss of forest area due to *jhuming* in Mizoram at 12 metric tonnes per hectare per year, thinks that the loss of forest cover due to the shifting cultivation in Mizoram is not substantial, as the way *jhuming* is practiced regenerates forests very quickly.[34]

Table 5.1 Shifting Cultivation in Northeastern States

State	Annual Area Under Shifting Cultivation (sq km)	Fallow Period (yr)	Minimum Area Under Shifting Cultivation at One Time or Another (sq km)	Number of Families Practicing Shifting Cultivation
Arunachal Pradesh	700	3-10	2,100	54,000
Assam	696	2-10	1,392	58,000
Manipur	900	4-7	3,600	70,000
Meghalaya	530	5-7	2,650	52,290
Mizoram	630	3-4	1,890	50,000
Nagaland	190	5-8	1,913	136,042
Tripura	223	5-9	1,115	43,000
Total Northeast	3,869 (1.5%)		14,660 (5.7%)	443,336

Source: Government of India, Ministry of Agriculture, *Task Force on Shifting Cultivation*, 1983.

When compared to the practice of settled cultivation, *jhum* cultivation, which does not involve ploughing and hoeing, contributes little to soil erosion. It is argued that *jhum* fires quickly render a dense forest fit for growing crops. Fire is thus a great labor-saving device that clears the jungle in a very short time. The ashes correct the soil activity, and the admixture of ashes with soil makes the soil more fertile. The soil on the hill slopes of high-rain zones is generally acidic. The alkali content of the ashes helps to neutralize them partially. The fire also clears the areas of extensive preponderance of fungi, insects, and pests.[35] Some other scholars have also pointed out that in steep hilly areas where communication is inadequate and sufficient land for terracing is not available, shifting cultivation becomes the only alternative that could provide livelihood to the majority of people in the hill areas with low levels of sociocultural and technological development and negligible proportion of level land.[36] Bhupinder Singh contends that *jhum* becomes indispensable owing to limits to the technology-absorption capacity of tribal communities.[37]

It is now more or less accepted that shifting cultivation is more of a human problem, hence it is spurious to examine the issue of shifting cultivation only from the environmental angle. Long back, in his work *The Baiga* (1939), Verrier Elwin exposed how restrictions imposed by the British on shifting cultivation reduced tribes to near-destitution and seriously eroded their culture, tradition, and sense of self-worth.[38] Scholars like P. C. Dutta and Tiplut Nongbri also point out that the transition from *jhuming* to settled cultivation leads to privatization of the community lands and increases economic inequalities, landlessness, reverse tenancy, indebtedness, insecurity, and hunger.[39] Thousands of *jhumis* have already lost their control over the *jhum* lands and become landless laborers. No efforts have been made to rehabilitate them as rehabilitation requires thousands of millions of rupees. Superficial compensation packages like distributing money or small plots of land will not help in protecting the food security of these communities. In the absence of viable alternatives, both on ecological and socio-cultural grounds most tribal peasants in the hills choose not to opt for sedentary farming.[40]

Forests, Economic Development, and Hill Tribes

The interdependence between forests and tribal communities is recognized by scholars as well as policy makers. Lack of access to plain lands and low levels of agricultural yield from shifting cultivation compel the hill communities to depend on forests for supplementing their material needs through hunting and food-gathering. During the colonial regime the British took over control of forests in mainland India and treated the tribal communities as encroachers. The plight of the tribals in the plains deteriorated as they were denied access to forests. But fortunately the tribal communities of the hills of composite Assam escaped the tragedy since the colonial authorities left control of forest areas in the hills to the tribal communities. After independence the Indian government also recognized the customary rights of the hill tribes of composite Assam over the land and forests and expected the ADCs constituted under the Sixth Schedule to ensure community control over the traditional resources.

The data on forest administration show that while the governments control over 80 percent of the forests in the country as a whole, in the northeastern region the protected and reserved forests put together account for only about 42 percent of the recorded forest area in the region. About 68 percent of the recorded forest area in the four tribal-dominant hill states of the northeast is unclassified, meaning outside the direct control of the state or central governments. The percentage of unclassified forests in Meghalaya and Nagaland is around 90 percent. The corresponding figures for Arunachal Pradesh, Mizoram, and

Assam are 62, 31 and 33 percent respectively.[41] Although governments are reluctant to recognize unclassified forests officially as community forests, much of what is declared as unclassified forests is in the hands of village authorities and local communities.

Table 5.2 Classification of Recorded Forest Area in
Northeastern Region

S. No.	State	Reserved Forest	Protected Forest	Unclassified Forest	Percentage of Unclassified Forests to Total Forest Area of State
1	Arunachal Pradesh	10,178	9,535	31,826	62
2	Assam	18,060	___	8,958	32
3	Manipur	1,467	4,171	11,780	68
4	Meghalaya	1,112	12	8,372	88
5	Mizoram	7,909	3,568	5,240	31
6	Nagaland	308	508	7,913	92
7	Tripura	3,588	554	2,041	32
	All India	399,919	238,434	136,387	17.6

Source: Forest Survey of India, *Report of State of Forests*, 2003.

Generally, it is assumed that when the forests are under the control of tribal communities they are protected better. But the data in the 1990s showed that the forest area in the northeastern region had actually declined. According to the *State of Forest Report* of 1999, between 1997 and 1999 forest cover in the northeast region declined by 642 sq km.

Compared to the all-India figure which illustrates the total decline of forest cover as only 244 sq km, the loss of forest cover in the northeastern region appeared to be quite substantial. The revelations of the report attracted the attention of several scholars, who were concerned about the loss of forest cover in the northeastern region.[42] Apart from shifting cultivation, many other factors such as increase of sedentary cultivation, logging, mining, cattle ranching and herding, and commercial tree plantations also contribute to the fall of forest cover. These factors apart the projects undertaken by governments in the name of infrastructure development, urban planning, and welfare are also found to have their own adverse effects on forests. In one study on the forest decline in the Garo Hills it was stated that construction of different types of roads has destroyed around 457 ha (hectares) of forest area.[43] Many express the fear that establishment of several new hydroelectric projects in the region as proposed would have adverse effects on the forests and biodiversity situation.

Some scholars attribute the decline of forest cover in the region to the wrong policies pursued by the ADCs and state governments. They point out that instead of upholding the customary rights of tribal communities over the forests the ADCs and state governments in the hill states have intruded on the rights of the tribal communities and taken direct or indirect control of the issues concerning the community forests. It is pointed out that in many respects the forest policies that these tribal-dominant hill states followed have remained only slightly modified versions of the laws applied in Assam and other states of India.[44] Recently, reviewing the status of community forests in the hill states, Community Forestry International, a US-based NGO, came out with suggestions for reviving and strengthening the same. Some of its recommendations included: (1)

strengthening of indigenous community institutions; (2) review of unclassified forests and official recognition of community forests; (3) mapping and delineation of borders of such community forests by involving the tribal communities; (4) updating the management skills of traditional institutions and tribal people in managing the forests by organizing workshops, seminars, and study tours for them; (5) giving proper orientation to the forest officials about the traditional tribal institutions, their traditions and customary rights; (6) demarcation and registration of community forests with ADCs to prevent encroachment by governments and private individuals; and (7) formulation of appropriate forest policies and programs keeping in mind the interests of indigenous people in the region.[45]

The national concern over decline of forest cover in the country as a whole led many NGOs to file Public Interest Litigation (PIL) suits seeking appropriate intervention by the courts. The Supreme Court of India gave an interim order in 1996 banning logging activities in the whole of the northeastern region. Indigenous organizations like the Khasi Students Union (KSU) in Meghalaya supported the court verdict. After the ban on logging the forest cover in the region has apparently improved to an extent. According to the *Report of State of Forests, 2003*, although shifting cultivation contributes to loss of forest cover, there has been an overall increase of about 2,400 sq km of the forest cover in the four tribal-dominant hill states in the northeast between 2001 and 2003.[46] Although the new report of the Forest Survey of India may be heartening to many there are some scholars who think differently. They point out that whereas the existing forest cover for the whole of India was only 20.64 percent in 2003 the corresponding figure for the seven northeastern states was over 73 percent.[47] Three hill states, namely, Arunachal Pradesh, Mizoram, and Nagaland

H. SRIKANTH

have forest cover of over 80 percent of their territories. The forest cover in Meghalaya is around 77 percent. Only in Assam is the forest cover just 35.48 percent, slightly above the stipulated national target. But even there it is sufficiently high in the two hill districts of Assam (Karbi-Anglong and North Cachar Hills). On the whole, the forest cover in all tribal areas of the northeast is well above the recommended level of 30 percent of the total area and 60 percent of the hill areas.

What the region lacks most is not forest cover but economic development. There are few industries in the region. As of March 2003 the total number of large and medium industries in the four tribal-dominant states of northeast India was only 82. The prospects of growth of small-scale industries in the hill states are also not that bright. Logging was the only industry providing employment to many locals and non-locals. The closure of the logging industries after the Supreme Court verdict had an adverse effect on the local economy. Commenting on this, Tiplut Nongbri raised a relevant question as to why the Indian state and courts are so concerned about forests in the northeast region when the forest cover in the region is considerably higher compared to the rest of India. Why is it that the northeastern region should pay the price for the inability of the rest of India to increase forest coverage? She argues that the obsession for conservation should not ignore the needs of development and livelihood of the indigenous people.[48] Many NGOs in the relatively underdeveloped West Khasi Hills District in Meghalaya share Nongbri's concerns. The growing concern for economic development in the region forces one to examine the experience of development strategies pursued in the region in recent years.

Development, Displacement, and Deprivation of Tribals

Legally speaking, the hill tribes living in the Sixth Schedule areas have control over resources like land, water, forests, mines, and so forth. All hill states and hill districts in the scheduled areas have enacted laws preventing transfer of lands from tribal to non-tribal people. Yet many scholars and activists have reported that alienation of tribal land has been taking place in indirect ways. In Karbi-Anglong, for example, the non-tribal cultivators – mostly the Biharis and the Nepalis – have obtained lands from tribal peasants on lease, taking advantage of reverse forms of tenancy prevalent in the district.[49] In and around Shillong the process of leasing lands to government organizations and individuals began as early as the colonial period. In her book, Nongbri has shown how colonial and post-colonial policies have activated the process of transformation of communal property of the Khasi community into private property and explained how the gradual accumulation of private property in the hands of a few of the tribal elite has started depriving the poor tribals of their access to communal resources.[50] In Mizoram, where the institution of chieftainship was replaced by village councils constituted by the state government, the communally-owned lands are clearly on the decline. In contrast, community lands appear to be protected better in Nagaland where the village councils consist of members chosen by the villagers in accordance with the prevailing customary practices and usage.[51]

A decade back scholars like Sukumaran Nair came to the conclusion that because of community ownership, depeasantization had not taken place on a large scale in Meghalaya.[52] But today there is considerable evidence to prove that a class of landless peasantry is emerging in the state, especially in the West Khasi Hills District, thanks to commercialization and privatization of agriculture. Although the customary laws could prevent the alienation of tribal lands to non-tribal people they have not been able to stop the increasing class differentiation within tribal communities. Further, in several urban pockets the non-tribals have started business in town areas collaborating with passive tribal partners who lack initiative and entrepreneurship. Non-tribal contractors, buyers, suppliers and wholesalers continue to have some hold over the local tribal economy. In fact, such a hold by the non-tribal elite from the plains is facilitated by the rise of tribal elite, dependent on non-tribal bureaucrats and businessmen from mainland India. Although the indigenous tribal elite are not favorably disposed toward competition from outsiders at the local level they do realize the need for forging links with business interests outside their respective states. The rise of educated middle classes and the birth of a rich indigenous propertied class has been the subject of several research articles and books on the northeast.[53] It was observed that much of the funds allocated to the region by the central government are pocketed by a small section of the indigenous elite. Hence, the need for appropriate interventions in the hills is increasingly being felt in recent years to ensure that the benefits of development reach the poor and needy among the tribals.

After independence the Indian state made the right political moves by incorporating the Fifth and Sixth Schedules as part of the Indian Constitution and assured the tribes of their customary rights over resources. But it is now increasingly becoming clear that the rights assured in the constitution are only conditional and that the Indian state continues to retain colonial laws that empower the state the right to take over even tribal lands in the name of public interest. In mainland India several dams, power projects and industries were started in tribal areas in the name of national development. Far from bringing benefits to the tribal people such developmental projects led to further misery, alienation and displacement (Table 5.3).[54]

Such kinds of development project–related human disasters are not confined to mainland India. The Gumti dam was built in Tripura, then a non-scheduled area, taking over 65 sq km of fertile land belonging to the tribal people.[55] In the state of Sikkim the government's proposals to build six hydroelectric projects along River Teesta to generate more than 3,000 MW of power has evoked considerable anxiety among the native people. In Manipur, ignoring the concerns expressed by certain tribal communities and environmentalist groups about displacement and environmental hazards, the government is going ahead with the Tipaimukh hydroelectric project in the hills of Manipur across the Barak river.[56] Of course, Sikkim state and the tribal areas of Manipur are not covered under the Sixth Schedule, but this has little to do with what is happening in the northeast in the name of development. No doubt the Sixth Schedule areas are better protected in this respect. Nevertheless, even here nothing stops governments from using the argument of pre-eminence of national interests to take possession of tribal lands. Taking defense and security of the nation as pretexts, thousands of acres of land have already been handed over to different military and paramilitary forces. In the name of tackling tribal insurgencies several villages were regrouped in Mizoram and Nagaland displacing the tribal people from their original habitats. In the 1960s the Assam government initiated the Umiam Hydro-Electric Project in the Khasi Hills and took over hundreds of square kilometers from the tribal communities without adequately compensating them. After the formation of Meghalaya the state government (now led by the in-

H. SRIKANTH

digenous tribal elite) initiated different projects that had adverse effects on the customary rights of hill tribes.

Table 5.3 Estimate of the Total Number of Persons and Tribals Displaced and Resettled by Various Development Projects in India during 1951-1990 (numbers in lakhs, i.e., hundreds of thousands)

Sl. No.	Type of Projects	Total			Tribal			% of Tribals to the Total	
		Dis-placed (No.)	Re-settled (No.)	% of coln. 4 over coln. 3	Dis-placed (No.)	Re-settled (No.)	% of coln. 7 over coln. 6	Dis-placed (coln. 6 over 3)	Resettled (coln. 7 over 4)
(1)	(2)	(3)	(4)	(5)	(6)	(7)	(8)	(9)	(10)
1	Dams	164.0	41.0	25.0	63.2	15.8	25.0	38.5	38.6
2	Mines	25.5	6.5	25.5	13.3	3.3	24.8	52.2	50.8
3	Indus-tries	12.5	3.8	30.4	3.1	0.8	25.8	25.0	21.1
4	Wildlife	6.0	1.3	21.7	4.5	1.0	22.2	75.0	77.0
5	Others	5.0	1.5	30.0	1.3	0.3	23.9	26.0	16.7
	Total	213.0	54.0	25.4	85.4	21.2	24.8	40.1	39.3

Source: Government of India, *Report of Steering Committee on Empowering the Scheduled Tribes for Tenth Five Year Plan,* 2002-07.

In recent years the Indian government has proposed to establish many more power projects in the northeastern region, including in the Sixth Schedule areas. It has been argued that with the commissioning of these projects the northeastern states would be able to generate 35,000 MW of electricity which they could sell to other Indian states and earn revenues. Supporting this point of view scholars like B. G. Verghese argue that developmental projects help in expanding infrastructure like roads, transport, and communications; generate adequate employment for the local people; and provide adequate resources to improve the living conditions of the people. It is held that since most of these projects are located in remote areas the costs of displacement will not be very high. The governments in the states have been trying to convince the people that economic prosperity ensured through such developmental projects and other initiatives like promotion of border trade and pursuit of the "Look East Policy" will weaken insurgency and ensure peace and harmony in the region.[57]

Such development prescriptions were, however, not received well by all. Many scholars and activists brought to light the adverse economic and social costs of the proposed development projects. It was pointed out that all major development projects involve acquisition of land that traditionally belongs to the tribals. Already, in the name of development projects and national parks, the state has taken possession of hundreds of acres of cultivable and *jhum* lands, depriving the tribal communities of their traditional sources of livelihood. The monetary compensation offered for such acquisitions is meager and insufficient to provide lifelong security. Profits that accrue from ventures such as power projects are usually pocketed by a few rich people.

Although development projects may ensure revenues for the state governments the poorer sections among the tribes gain little since most of these projects offer few employment opportunities for the locals who are mostly unskilled. Even where some jobs are reserved for the locals it is observed that most jobs offered to the tribals remain at the lower rungs of the official hierarchy. Since mega-projects need technically-skilled laborers the native communities apprehend large-scale immigration of thousands of non-tribal people into these tribal areas. In the northeast there have been instances where some tribal communities displaced by such development projects migrated to other

H. SRIKANTH

states, causing ethnic tensions in the host states.[58] Apart from ethnic tensions, many scholars and activists have also focused on the environmental and cultural loss of the proposed projects like dams and uranium mining. In Tripura the tribals whose lands were submerged with the commissioning of the Gumti project have taken to shifting cultivation on the hills, endangering the forests.[59] Many environmental groups express the fear that if the proposed hundreds of dams and power projects in Arunachal Pradesh really materialize they will not only imperil the habitats of endangered species but also submerge thousands of hectares of land, including some towns, and displace more than 30,000 people. Much of the social and environmental costs of the projects are indirectly borne by the poor tribals. In Sikkim tunneling and blasting have caused landslides and springs have started drying up. The locals there complain of the muck and rock debris dumped in the river and express fear that the entry of thousands of migrant workers would swamp the local culture of the Buddhist, Christian, and animist Lepchas.

The indigenous people are organizing themselves against many of these proposed projects. There is growing demand now in Tripura for decommissioning the Gumti project and redistribution of the reclaimed land to the tribals. In Arunachal Pradesh the people have been opposing the Subansiri and Dihing dams citing displacement, forest loss and submersion of six major townships including Along, Daporizo, and Yinkiong. In Sikkim, due to popular pressure the government was forced to withdraw a project in the sacred valley of Rathong Chu honoring the sentiments, religion, and culture of the people of Sikkim. For similar reasons the tribal people in the hills of Manipur are fighting against the proposed Tipaimukh project. In Meghalaya, despite the government's efforts to convince them of the benefits of the project the majority of the people have opposed uranium mining. Although there is no opposition to commissioning of hydroelectric projects in Meghalaya the indigenous tribes are demanding that their community and regional interests and aspirations be taken care of and that only competent firms be given contracts for completion of the projects. Criticizing the indigenous people's objections and demands apologists of development projects say such movements are uninformed and anti-development. But as one Bamang Anthony of Arunachal Citizens Rights says, "Promoters are talking development. We also want development but we want to know what kind of development they want in our land. There is no transparency." The native activists allege that despite a large number of projects on the anvil the governments have miserably failed to provide facts on how they would be commissioned.[60] The indigenous participants of different regional meetings on Dams and Development in the Northeast, therefore, resolved that their decisions regarding future dam projects in the region must be preceded by answers to the following questions:

1. Have the development needs and objectives been formulated through an open and participatory process at local and regional levels?

2. Has a comprehensive options assessment for water and energy resource development been done?

3. Have the social and environmental factors been given the same significance as techno-economic aspects in assessing options?

4. Do we have a basin-wide understanding of the ecology of the rivers and the dependence of local communities on them?[61]

As such, the native opposition to the development projects has its roots in experience and also in the lack of transparency. Today most indigenous hill communities of the northeast have become sufficiently organized and politicized. They would not passively approve any development proposals unless they are fully convinced that the projects are beneficial to them. It is the responsibility of governments to provide full information to the indigenous peoples, apprise them of the possible fallouts, and convince them of the benefits that the projects would bring to the tribal peoples and their habitats. It is, therefore, necessary that the indigenous peoples be involved at all levels of the commissioning of the project, from the stage of planning to implementation to their appraisal.

Conclusion

Unlike Canada, Australia, and New Zealand, which have started talking about aboriginal self-governments only in recent decades, the Government of India has been experimenting with different forms of tribal self-governments since India attained independence. The Fifth and Sixth Schedules of the Indian Constitution made provisions for ensuring the autonomy and economic development of the tribal areas. When the ADCs failed to satisfy the tribals' aspirations for autonomy, the Government of India conceded even state (provincial) status to the tribal-dominant districts of composite Assam. Considering the fact that no region inhabited by the aboriginal peoples in Canada and other advanced liberal democratic states has attained the status of a province, the formation of tribal-dominant states in India was indeed a great step forward toward aboriginal self-government. However, the review of the working of ADCs and tribal state governments in northeast India shows that these constitutional institutions have not risen to the expectations of tribal communities.

The structures and functioning of the tribal governments did not qualitatively differ from liberal political institutions. No doubt the new institutions helped the emerging indigenous tribal elite to rise in the administrative and political hierarchies, but there was little that the poor tribals got out of them. Although the tribal governments could prevent non-tribal exploitation to an extent, they could not check the growing class differences within the tribal communities. Having to work in a liberal capitalist framework the tribal governments could do little to arrest the process of privatization of community lands. With vested interests growing within, different development projects which appear to be detrimental to the interests of the majority are initiated in the name of economic development. Growth of tribal population, gradual decline of communal property, and expansion of educational opportunities have given birth to unemployed tribals seeking jobs outside the traditional sectors. But with no viable alternatives emerging, the indigenous peoples in the hill areas of northeast India find themselves situated between the Devil and the deep sea.

Notes and References

1. G. S. Ghurye, *The Burning Caldron of North-East India* (Bombay: Popular Prakashan, 1980), 52-122.
2. Verrier Elwin, "Issues in Tribal Policy Making," in *Tribe, Caste and Religion in India*, ed. Romesh Thapar (Delhi: Macmillan Publishing, 1977), 29–37; and also his *Tribal World of Verrier Elwin: An Autobiography* (New Delhi: Oxford University Press, 1998). For a comprehensive understanding of Verrier Elwin's contributions, refer Ramachandra Guha, *Savaging the Civilized: Verrier Elwin, His Tribals and India* (Delhi: Oxford University Press, 1999).
3. For Nehru's Panchsheel for Tribals, see his "Foreword" to Verrier Elwin's *Philosophy of NEFA*. Also refer Govinda Chandra Rath, ed., *Tribal Development in India: The Contemporary Debate* (New Delhi: Sage Publications, 2006).
4. Amir Hasan, *Tribal Administration in India* (New Delhi: B. R. Publishing).
5. SCs are untouchable castes occupying inferior status in the caste hierarchy. As against the SCs, the STs are tribes who are outside the purview of the caste hierarchy.
6. Ministry of Tribal Welfare, *Annual Report 2004–05* (New Delhi: Government of India, 2005).
7. D. V. Kumar, "Tribal Development: Issues, Movements and Interventions," *Sociologist* 1:1 (March 2007): 101–3; B.K. Roy Burman, "Constitutional Framework for Tribal Autonomy for Tribal Autonomy with Special Reference to North-East India," in *North-East India: The Human Interface*, ed. M. K. Raha and Aloke Kumar Ghosh (New Delhi: Gyan Publishing, 1998).
8. V. Venkat Rao, *Tribal Politics in North-East India 1874–1974* (Delhi: S. Chand, 1976), 257–303.

9. L. S. Gassah, "Traditional System of Governance among the Khasis, Jaintias and Garos of Meghalaya and the Changes thereof," in *Polity and Economy: Agenda for Contemporary North-East India*, ed. C. Joshua Thomas (New Delhi: Regency Publications, 2005), 82-9; R. N. Prasad, "Sixth Schedule and Working of the District Councils in North-Eastern States," *Dialogue* 6:2 (October–December 2004), www.asthabharati.org/Dia_Oct04/prasad.htm accessed 12 December 2007.

10. B. K. Roy Burman, "Sixth Schedule of the Constitution," in *Autonomous District Councils*, ed. L. S. Gassah (New Delhi: Omsons Publications, 1997), 33.

11. Rao, *Tribal Politics*, 298.

12. Prasad, "Sixth Schedule."

13. R. N. Prasad, *Autonomous Movements in Mizoram* (Delhi: Vikas Publishing, 1994).

14. David Syiemlieh, "Traditional Institutions of Governance in the Hills of North-East India: The Khasi Experience," *Man and Society: A Journal of North-East Studies* 3 (Spring 2006): 131.

15. Refer S. K. Chaubey, *Hill Politics in Northeast India* (New Delhi: Orient Longman, 1999); Dhiren Bhagawati, "Meghalaya: The Struggle of the Three Sisters to Have a Place in the Sun," in *Political Dynamics of Northeast India*, ed. Girin Phukon (New Delhi: South Asian Publishers, 2000), 175-186; C. Nunthara, *Mizoram: Society and Polity* (New Delhi: Indus Publishing, 1996); R. N. Prasad, *Government and Politics in Mizoram* (New Delhi: Northern Book Centre, 1987).

16. Tiplut Nongbri, *Development, Ethnicity and Gender* (New Delhi: Rawat Publications, 2003), 146.

17. P. S. Dutta, *Autonomous Movements in Assam* (New Delhi: Omsons Publishing, 1993).

18. H. Srikanth and Joshua C. Thomas, "Naga Resistance Movement and the Peace Process in North-East India," in *Peace in India's North-East: Meaning, Metaphor and Method*, ed. Presenjit Biswas and C. Joshua Thomas (New Delhi: Regency, 2006), 361.

19. Ashish Kothari, "The Khonoma Magic: A Nagaland Village Leads the Way," Kalpavriksh Environment Action Group, www.kalpavriksh.org/f3/regnagaland/Khonoma%20for%20Hindu%20Survey%20final%2012.3.2005.doc accessed 12 December 2004; Hiren Gohain, "An Example from Nagaland," *Assam Tribune* (Guwahati, 20 December 2007), http://www.assamtribune.com/scripts/details.asp?id=dec2007/edit2 accessed 12 December 2007.

20. B. D. Sharma, "Reassertion by the Community in the Tribal Areas," *Dialogue* 3:2 (October–December 2001), http://www.asthabharati.org/Dia_Oct01/reassertion.htm accessed 12 December 2007; also B. K. Roy Burman, "Constitutional Framework for Tribal Autonomy with Special Reference to North-East India," in *North-East India: The Human Interface*, ed. M. K. Raha and Aloke Kumar Ghosh (New Delhi: Gyan Publishing, 1998), 91–2.

21. Sharma, ibid.

22. Syiemlieh, "Traditional Institutions," 129–30.

23. Bengst Karlsson, "Sovereignty through Indigenous Governance: Reviving 'Traditional Political Institutions' in Northeast India," *NEHU Journal* III:2 (2005): 1–15.

24. Refer *A Consultation Paper on Empowering and Strengthening of Panchayati Raj Institutions/Autonomous District Councils/Traditional Tribal Governing Institutions in North-East India* (New Delhi: National Commission to Review the Working of the Constitution, 2001), 32.

25. Rajesh Dev, A. K. Baruah and Manorama Sharma, "Liberal Democracy, Traditional Institutions and Politics of Representation: Analysing the Nongkynrih Shnong Dorbar," Crises States Program, London School of Economics, www.crisisstates.com/download/projectnotes/dev_baruah_sharma.pdf accessed 12 December 2004.

26. Apurba K. Baruah, "Tribal Traditions and Crises of Governance in North-East India, with Special Reference to Meghalaya," Crises States Program, London School of Economics, Working Paper No. 22, March 2003, 6, http://www.crisisstates.com/download/wp/WP22AB.pdf accessed 12 December 2007.

27. Manorama Sharma, "Critically Assessing Traditions: The Case of Meghalaya," Crises States Program, London School of Economics, Working Paper No. 52, November 2004, http://www.crisisstates.com/download/wp/wp52.pdf accessed 12 December 2007.

28. Apurba K. Baruah, "Ethnic Conflicts and Traditional Self-Governing Institutions: A Study of Laitumukhrah Dorbar," Crisis States Program, London School of Economics, Working Paper No. 39, January 2004, 19, http://www.crisisstates.com/download/wp/wp39.pdf accessed 12 December 2007.

29. Syiemlieh, "Traditional Institutions," 132–3; also Toki Blah, "Traditional Institutions and Urban Governance," *Shillong Times*, 3 and 4 May 2004.

30. Government of India, North-Eastern Council, *Basic Statistics of NER 2006* (Shillong: NEC Secretariat, 2007), 171.

31. Anup Saikia, "Indigenous Control and Sustainability of Common Resources in the Hills of North-East India," http://www.gdnet.org/fulltext/saikia.pdf accessed 12 December 2007; Naresh C. Saxena, "National Draft Policy on Tribals: Suggestions for Improvement," National Advisory Council, Government of India, http://nac.nic.in/concept%20papers/draft_goi_tribal.pdf accessed 12 December 2007.

32. Saxena, ibid.

33. Verrier Elwin, *A Philosophy for NEFA* (Shillong: NEFA Administration, 1959).

34. Daman Singh, *Last Frontier: People and Forests in Mizoram* (Delhi: Tata Energy Research Institute, 1991).

35. A. K. Sinha, B. G. Banerjee and R. N. Vashisht, "Shifting Cultivation in North-Eastern India: A Way of Life," *Man & Development* (March 2004): 79.

36. Debojyoti Das, "Demystifying the Myth of Shifting Cultivation Agronomy in the North-East," *Economic and Political Weekly* 41:46 (5 November 2006): 4912–17.

37. Bhupinder Singh, "Perspective and Plans," in *Socio-Economic and Ecological Development*, ed. Bhuddadeb Chaudhuri (New Delhi: Inter-India Publications, 1992), 2.

38. Verrier Elwin, *The Baiga* (New Delhi: Gian Publishers, 1991 edn.).

39. See P.S. Dutta, India's North-East: A Study in Transition (Delhi: Vikas, 1992); also Nongbri, *Development*, 140–2.

40. Manju Menon, Kanchi Kohli and Neeraj Vagholikar, "Em'power'ing the Northeast," Environment Action Group, www.kalpavriksh.org/f1/f1.3/Hindu%20Survey%202003,%20NE%20dams,%20KK%20MM%20NV%2028.2.2002,%20final.doc accessed 12 December 2007.

41. *Basic Statistics of NER 2006*, 173.
42. Saikia, "Indigenous Control": also R. Ranjan and V. P. Upadhyay, "Ecological Problems due to Shifting Cultivation," *Current Science 77* (1999): 1246–50; S. Sarma, "Shifting Cultivation in
Meghalaya," *North-Eastern Geographer* 19 (1987): 61–9.
43. S. K. Bera, S. K. Basumatary, A. Agarwal and M. Ahmed, "Con-
version of Forest Land in Garo Hills, Meghalaya for Construction of
Roads: A Threat to the Environment and Biodiversity,"
www.ias.ac.in/currsci/aug102006/281.pdf accessed 12 December 2007.
44. Nongbri, *Development*, 142–5.
45. Mark Poffenberger, ed., *Indigenous Forest Stewards of Northeast
India* (California: Community Forestry International, 2004), 81–90,
http://www.communityforestryinternational.org/pdfs/Indige-
nous_Forest_Stewards_of_NE_India.pdf accessed 12 December 2007.
46. *Basic Statistics of NER 2006*, 174.
47. Forest Survey of India, *State of Forest Report, 2003* (Dehradun:
Forest Survey of India), 2004.
48. Tiplut Nongbri, "Timber Ban in North-East India: Effects on
Livelihood and Gender," *Economic and Political Weekly* 36:21 (26
May 2001): 1893–900.
49. *Report of the Survey of Alienation of Tribal Land in Assam* (Guwahati: Assam Institute of Research on Tribals and Scheduled Castes,
1999), 27–30; also B. N. Bordoloi, *Transfer and Alienation of Tribal
Land in Assam with Special Reference to the Karbis of the Karbi-Anglong
District* (Guwahati: Western Book Depot, 1991).
50. Nongbri, *Development*, 129.
51. According to a Forest Sector Review of North-East India, the
community forests in Nagaland and Meghalaya amount respectively
to 91 and 90 percent of the total forested area in the state. The corresponding figure for Mizoram is only 33 percent. Refer Poffenberger,
Indigenous Forest Stewards, 22; see also N. K. Dash, "Agrarian Structure and Change in Nagaland," in *Economies of the Tribes and their
Transition*, ed., K. S. Singh (New Delhi: Concept Publishing, 1982),
314–18.
52. M. K . Sukumaran Nair, *Tribal Economy in Transition: A Study of
Meghalaya* (New Delhi: Inter-India Publications, 1987), 141–7.

53. Refer B. Datta Ray, *The Emergence and Role of Middle Class in North-East India* (Delhi: Uppal Publishing, 1983); Manorama Sharma, *Social and Economic Change in Assam: Middle Class Hegemony* (Delhi: Ajanta Publishers, 1990); A. K. Baruah, *Social Tensions in Assam: Middle Class Politics* (Guwahati: Purbanchal Publishing, 1991); Sanjib Baruah, *India Against Itself: Assam and the Politics of Identity* (New Delhi: Oxford University Press, 2001); Sajal Nag, *Contesting Marginality: Ethnicity, Insurgency and Subnationalism in North-East India* (Delhi: Manohar Publishers, 2002).

54. Walter Fernandez, ed., *National Development and Tribal Deprivation* (New Delhi: Indian Social Institute, 1992); Ravi Hemadri, "Dams, Displacement, Policy and Law in India," World Commission on Dams, www.dams.org/docs/kbase/contrib/soc213.pdf> accessed 12 December 2007; Amrita Patwardhan, "Dams and Tribal People in India," paper contributed to the World Commission on Dams, http://www.dams.org/docs/kbase/contrib/soc207.pdf accessed 12 December 2007; Ghanshyam Shah, "Tribal Issues: Problems and Prospects," in *Tribal Transformation in India*, vol. 2, ed. B. Chaudhuri (Delhi: Inter-India Publications, 1982), 113–41.

55. Malaya Banerjee, "Gumti Hydel Project and Displaced Persons" in *Blisters on their Feet: Tales of Internally Displaced Persons in India's Northeast*, ed. Samir Kumar Das (Delhi: Sage Publications, 2008).

56. Subir Bhaumik, "The Dam and the Tribal," *Himal South Asian*, May 2004, www.himalmag.com/2004/may/perspective.htm accessed 12 December 2007; Simon Denyer, "Indian Plan to Dam Northeast Rivers Stirs Critics," http://www.planetark.com/avantgo/dailynewsstory.cfm?newsid=36919 accessed 12 December 2007.

57. B. G. Verghese, "The Bounty of North-Eastern Waters," in *Challenges of Development in North-East India*, ed. Anuradha Datta, David R. Syiemlieh and Srinath Barua (New Delhi: Regency Publications, 2006), 192–207.

58. Walter Fernandez, "Development Displaced and the Right to Life: Implications for the Northeast," in *Problems of Internally Displaced Persons in Assam with Special Reference to Barak Valley*, ed. Tanmoy Bhattacharjee (Silchar: Assam University, 2003), 3–27, http://www.creighton.edu/CollaborativeMinistry/NESRC/Walter/AUSPAPER.doc accessed 12 December 2007.

59. Subir Bhaumik, "Land Reclaim Dispute over Drying Dam," BBC, http://news.bbc.co.uk/2/hi/south_asia/6509771.stm accessed 12 December 2007.
60. Richnel Mahapatra, "At NE Cost: Power for All, Provider Largely Northeast," *Down to Earth* 12:9 (30 September 2003): 6.
61. Menon, Kohli and Vagholikar, "Em'power'ing the Northeast."

H. Srikanth

6

CONCLUSION

In the context of increasing global attention that the aboriginal peoples' movements have been receiving in recent decades, this book has made an attempt to understand the journeys of indigenous communities in two countries: Canada and India. Canada is ranked as one among the developed countries in the world today, whereas India is still a developing country. Yet, the two countries have certain similarities. Features such as a colonial British past, multicultural social fabric, liberal democratic constitutions, federalism, welfare capitalism, and a parliamentary form of government are common to both countries. Despite their emergence as liberal modern nation states both countries have some segments of population which could not thus far fully identify and integrate themselves with the nations in whose territorial boundaries they are located by virtue of the latter holding overwhelming state power. Apart from communities like the Francophones in Canada and the Kashmiris in India which have made their presence felt as distinct nationalities, both countries have aboriginal populations which have been living in the territories for centuries prior to the emergence of Canada and India as nation states.

These aboriginal communities seeking recognition as indigenous peoples or as First Nations could not be drawn into capitalist modernity despite attempts made by colonial and post-colonial regimes to assimilate them into the national mainstream. Although the state elite look at them primarily as tribes or bands which are backward and need to be civilized and developed, the communities themselves take pride in their aboriginal/tribal identities and oppose efforts aimed at mainstreaming them. As original/first settlers they invoke the right to self-determination and seek protection and preservation of their languages, cultures, and traditions through self-government. They have been organizing themselves into political parties, pressure groups, and militant organizations and fighting for restoration of their traditional rights over lands and resources.

Focusing on the FN communities in the Canadian province of British Columbia (BC) and the hill tribes of composite Assam the present book has sought to comprehend the colonial experiences of the indigenous communities and the nature and forms of native struggles in two entirely different settings. The book also sought to appreciate the changing policies of the governments in Canada and India toward the indigenous peoples fighting for recognition and restoration of aboriginal rights. The book has also reviewed different debates on native self-governments and reflected on the limitations and prospects of aboriginal governments operating within the bounds of liberal democratic nation states. Since the history of indigenous peoples took different trajectories, they have been studied separately. Having gained insights into the native situation in Canada and India, this concluding chapter will focus on similarities and dissimilarities in indigenous peoples' problems, struggles, and achievements in the two regions.

Similarities between FNs of Canada and Hill Tribes of India's Northeast

At the very outset, one needs to clarify as to what is similar between the FNs in BC and the hill tribes of north-

H. SRIKANTH

east India that merits study. Given the prevailing controversies over who constitute indigenous peoples, one could even question the rationale behind viewing the hill tribes as indigenous peoples. In Canada, where there has been continuity between colonial and post-colonial regimes all communities that existed prior to the arrival of European settlers are treated as aboriginals and indigenous peoples. This apparently clear criterion, however, poses difficulties for countries like India, which witnessed a series of immigrations in its thousands of years of history. Considering the facts that all communities inhabiting the Indian subcontinent prior to the British contact were not aboriginals and that the colonial rule had differential impacts on the tribal and non-tribal communities in the country, this book took the stand that only the tribal communities which remained peripheral and marginal in the colonial and post-colonial regimes could be viewed as indigenous communities, irrespective of whether they were the first settlers of the land they presently occupy or not. It is only when one takes the positional criterion that one can see similarities between the hill tribes of the erstwhile composite Assam and the FNs in BC.

As stated at the beginning, self-representation is one of the key determinants in identifying indigenous peoples. Both the FNs in Canada and hill communities in northeast India consider themselves indigenous people and view other peoples who migrated to their territories after the British colonization as outsiders. Economically, these communities are not part of the modern capitalistic system and demographically they are national minorities. These communities view themselves and are also identified by others, including the governments, as tribal people. Although touched by the forces of modernity many of the characteristic features of a tribe are absent in both the sets of communities and, culturally, they can be distinguished from more advanced communities. Notions of modernity, nation state, individual rights, common citizenship, capitalism, and rule of law are still alien to their cultures. Their movements, which normally take ethnic or communitarian forms, revolve primarily around issues of identity, autonomy, and protection of aboriginal rights. The indigenous peoples are opposed to the colonial model of development although they are not averse to social change and progress. They seek development that is compatible with their traditions, culture, environment, and communitarian beliefs.[1]

Structural and Geographical Differences

These apparent similarities should not lead us to ignore the differences between the FNs and the hill tribes. Although both are demographic minorities in their respective countries the indigenous hill communities in northeast India constitute more than 80 percent of the population in the three hill states and are around two-thirds in a fourth hill state. But FNs make up less than 10 percent of the population in all provinces of Canada, barring Saskatchewan. Only in the Northwest Territories do the First Nations constitute about 36 percent of the population. In 2006 the total aboriginal population in Canada, including the Metis and the Inuit, crossed the one million mark, whereas the indigenous tribal population in the state of Nagaland alone was over one million in 1991.[2] Further, the territories that hill tribes inhabit in northeast India are contiguous and much larger compared to the reserves allotted to the FNs in Canada. North Cachar Hills District in the state of Assam inhabited by hill tribes like the Dimasas, Kukis, Karbis, and others is around 4,890 sq km whereas the state of Arunachal Pradesh which is host to several indigenous tribes is 83,743 sq km. In contrast,

H. SRIKANTH

even the largest reserves allotted to the FNs in Canada are only around 1,300 sq km. It is only in recent decades that treaty negotiations are on to settle the land claims and ensure an adequate land base for Indian self-governments. The Nisga'a community in BC secured control over territory measuring 1,900 sq km through the Nisga'a Treaty in 2000.[3] If culturally- and linguistically-related FN communities join together they could negotiate self-governments whose jurisdiction could extend over large territories. But conflict of interests often prompts them to negotiate separate treaties. One witnessed something similar in northeast India as well. In view of geographical contiguity, it was possible for the hill tribes of northeast India to have one or two big states. As discussed earlier, initially, in the 1950s and early 1960s several hill tribes of composite Assam organized united movements for a separate hill state. Later, internal contradictions compelled them to continue their fight for autonomy either separately as in the case of Mizos, or in combination with like-minded communities as was the case with the Khasis, Jaintias, and Garos. Tribal states that came into existence thereafter may be smaller in area compared to many other states in mainland India, but there is hardly an FN territory in Canada which is as big as, say Nagaland, the smallest hill state in northeast India, measuring 16,579 sq km.

Colonial Experiences of Indigenous Peoples

Unlike the FNs in BC, who traditionally thrived on occupations like fishing and hunting for their livelihood, for centuries almost all hill tribes in the northeast depended primarily on agriculture, mostly on shifting or terrace cultivation and adopted primitive methods of cultivation. This variation has more to do with ecology and availability of resources than with any mechanical evolutionary notions of human development. Their traditional ways of living underwent considerable changes after the British colonization. Under the colonial rule the FNs in BC suffered much more compared to the hill communities in composite Assam. The FNs lost control over their traditional territories to the white immigrants and were subjected to all kinds of discrimination. Efforts were made to extinguish their aboriginal rights and identities.[4] In contrast, after the consolidation of their authority over frontier areas of northeast India, the British enacted different Acts with a view to protecting the hill communities from the traders and planters from the plains. The colonial authorities chose not to introduce any radical administrative and economic changes and relied considerably on the traditional tribal chiefs to run the day-to-day administration. The creation of separate districts for hill communities and the restrictions imposed on the people from the plains from entering the hill areas facilitated the development of ethnic consciousness among the indigenous hill communities.[5]

During the colonial period, Christian missionaries played a very important role in the lives of FNs and hill tribes. Although they cannot be branded as agents of colonialism, one cannot deny the fact that the missionaries in BC as well as in hill areas of composite Assam helped the colonizers to establish their cultural and political supremacy over the aboriginal communities. However, unlike Canada where the FNs detested the missionaries for destroying their native traditions and culture and for leaving deep scars in their minds of their experience in compulsory residential schools, the hill tribes in northeast India see Christian missionaries as saviors who elevated them from savagery and brought about changes in their lives through education and the gospel. In one sense, Christian-

H. SRIKANTH

ity became a sort of marker for the indigenous hill communities in northeast India to distinguish themselves from the predominantly Hindu population of mainland India. Such identification with Christianity could not take place in Canada since their adversaries, the white colonizers, themselves are Christians. Although the majority of FNs in Canada accepted Christianity, the natives continue to criticize the missionaries for the damage they did to their culture and psyche.[6]

Native Struggles in Post-Colonial Regimes

When seen from the viewpoint of the aboriginal Indians, in North America there is no clear-cut distinction between the colonial and the post-colonial regimes. Even after the formation of the Canadian federation in 1864, colonial and racist policies toward the FNs continued for several decades in BC and other Canadian provinces. Hence, the political objectives of the FN movement remained more or less the same before and also after the birth of Canada. The aboriginal Indians insist on recognition of their distinct identity as First Nations and demand that the Canadian state stop all policies of assimilation. Most FN groups in Canada maintain that their right to self-determination should be recognized, but are pragmatic enough to realize that demographic factors and other structural constraints make secession from Canada an impossible option. They understand that they do not have a future outside Canada and all that they can fight for is for self-government within Canada with substantial powers to shape the future of their people in the manner they like.

The tribal situation in the hills of composite Assam is different from the FN experience in Canada. Although it took several decades for the British to suppress tribal revolts, once annexation was complete the hill tribes more or less accepted the British authority. Thanks to the role of the Christian missionaries, some tribes began to see British rule as a blessing-in-disguise. Because of the colonial policy of keeping the hills insulated from the rest of India, the hill communities found it difficult to identify themselves with mainland Indians and their anti-colonial struggle. Hence, when the British chose to leave the country, the indigenous communities were in a dilemma and state of shock. The hill tribes did not have the material base to emerge as independent nations. But at the same time, they had their own apprehensions about joining the Indian Union, as it was primarily conceived and shaped by the Indian nationalist elite. The manner in which the hill areas were integrated with the Indian Union and the subsequent failure of the Indian state in addressing the aspirations and concerns of the hill communities gave birth to different tribal movements in the hills. Political movements of the hill communities in the post-independence period were directed against the Indian state either with the idea of seceding from India, or for attaining greater autonomy for themselves within the Indian Union. In both cases, the intended political objective was to preserve their distinct political and cultural identities and to resist the real or perceived threats of exploitation, assimilation, or domination by the Indian elite.

Indigenous Peoples' Movements: Strategies and Tactics

FN movements in Canada took recourse to legal and political forms of struggle and even when they mobilized a large number of people in pursuit of their demands, by and large the native organizations adopted peaceful constitutional means. By lobbying through international fo-

H. SRIKANTH

rums and organizations working for indigenous people they succeeded in exercising pressure on the Canadian state to accede to their demands. Instances where FNs took to violence are few and usually followed by engagements and intense negotiations with the governments.

Contrarily, from the very beginning the tribal movements in the hill areas of northeast India witnessed two trends – one of militant violence, and the other of mass political movement. In the 1950s and 1960s the Nagas took to insurrectionary means to achieve independence, while the Khasis, Jaintias, and Garos adopted mass movements to achieve their demand for a separate tribal state within the Indian Union. The distinction between militancy and mass movement has, however, become blurred in recent decades, with many tribal organizations in the hills taking to both means to achieve their ends. Earlier, violence was directed primarily against the state and military personnel. But in recent decades several tribal organizations have resorted to road blockades, physical attacks on non-tribal people, *bandhs*, kidnappings, murders, extortion and strikes, and harassment. The outcomes of such radical postures failed to achieve anything positive. The growing tribal militancy in the hills could, in fact, accomplish little in recent years compared to what the mass political movements of the hill communities could achieve in the 1950s and 1960s. In a way the mindless violence that some tribal militant groups indulge in add to the people's insecurity and distance them from such organizations and movements. Forced displacement of ethnic minorities and killing of innocent civilians by indigenous militant organizations helped the Indian state to justify deployment and use of the Armed Forces by projecting the indigenous peoples' struggles as terrorist plots. Of late, as nations around the world have started endorsing the US-initiated fight against terror, external material support to the militant indigenous organizations in northeast India has come down drastically. Thus, in a way the growth of ethnic militancy has weakened the indigenous peoples' movements in the hills of northeast India.

Conflicting claims over the same territories by two or more communities claiming to be indigenous also weaken the indigenous peoples' movements. This problem is less intense in Canada where the FN communities are widely dispersed and instances where more than one community laying claim for the same territory are not many. But in the hill areas of northeast India where several tribes inhabit the same territories, their struggles for creating ethnic homelands for taking control of land and other resources at times get complicated as their overlapping claims over particular territories often end up in violent inter-ethnic conflicts.[7] In such situations, the ethnic other is perceived as the more important enemy than the Indian state. When indigenous peoples' movements degenerate into ethnic conflicts, they create opportunities for the state to play one community against another.

Response of the Liberal Democratic States

The indigenous peoples' movements and campaigns exposed the plight of indigenous peoples in modern nation states and showed to the world the darker side of "liberal" democracies. By effectively indicting the theory and practice of classical liberalism they compelled the liberal elite to come to terms with ideas of multiculturalism and communitarianism. Compelled by the indigenous peoples' movements and struggles liberal democratic states like Canada had to take cognizance of the existence of aboriginal rights and change their approach and attitudes toward the native problem. In recent decades treaty negotiations have been taking place in Canada to settle land claims and give shape to Indian self-government. But to this day there is no FN territory in Canada that enjoys the status of a province. The Northwest Territories in Canada have a considerable FN population, but it does not enjoy provincial status. No doubt the ratification of the Nunavut Act in 1993, guaranteeing self-government for Inuit is a great step towards aboriginal self-government, but Nunavut is only a territory and does not enjoy the status as a province of Canada. In contrast, the Indian Constitution made provision for the Sixth Schedule, guaranteeing autonomy to the indigenous tribal communities inhabiting the hill districts of composite Assam. Later the Indian government went to the extent of conceding state status to certain tribal-dominant territorial units. But from the very beginning, the Indian state has outrightly rejected all kinds of secessionist demands and insisted that all solutions must be sought within the framework of the Indian Constitution. The Indian state did not hesitate to use repression against indigenous people's movements, especially when they took the shape of insurgency and threatened the territorial integrity of the Indian nation state. It is often alleged that the Armed Forces involved in anti-insurgency operations have indulged in several instances of blatant violations of human rights.

In this respect the Canadian record fares better. One could argue that the need for state repression did not arise in Canada since the FN movements consciously chose not to insist on sovereignty or independence. At another level it could also be argued that being a developed capitalist country Canada has adequate physical and financial resources to accommodate the reasonable aspirations of the FNs. The Canadian state could, therefore, avoid coercive mechanisms while dealing with the FN challenge. Contrar-

ily, being an underdeveloped country lacking adequate resources to satisfy all discontented communities, the Indian
state's capacities to deal with tribal movements without repression are limited. Violent inter-ethnic conflicts also compel the Indian state to use force to bring peace in the region.
But arguments such as lack of resources and ethnic conflicts
cannot justify continuous use of force against all indigenous
peoples' movements. Inhuman violence perpetrated in the
1950s and 1960s against the Nagas and the Mizos was basically engendered by the arrogance of the state elite in India
which could not tolerate small tribes daring to challenge
the national might of India. Violations of human rights in
insurgency-prone areas are not mere aberrations: they were
deliberate acts by the state meant to teach lessons to those
communities which think and act differently. But such state
repression, far from putting an end to tribal militancy, created yet more aversion in the minds of indigenous hills peoples and perpetuated anti-India feelings.

Even in Canada the FNs underwent inhuman forms
of oppression and discrimination for centuries. But in recent decades the Canadian state has been making amends
to erase the bitter memories of the past. Of all positive steps
that the Canadian state has taken the one that helped most
in paving the way for peace and reconciliation was the
Canadian government's open admission of its past mistakes.
The governments and the Church in Canada apologized ex-
plicitly to the aboriginal communities for their inhuman
acts of the past in their attempts to assimilate the indigenous
peoples.[8] The Indian state could as well pave the way for a
process of genuine peace by making a candid apology and
shunning the use of force against innocent civilians. It came
close to this when former Prime Minister Atal Bihari Va-
japayee acknowledged the distinct history of the Nagas and
pleaded for a continuation of political dialogue for an hon-

orable solution to the Naga problem. While admitting that a lot of people suffered, wheels of development stopped and mistakes committed, he said that rather than remaining tied to the past, "we have to take care of the present and look to the future."[9] Although pragmatism demands such overtures, the dominant state ideology of "One state, one nation" makes it difficult for the Indian state to admit that smaller ethnic communities or sub-nationalities in the country also have the right to self-determination and that they need to be won over through reason and love, not repression and domination.

Future of Indigenous Peoples' Governments

As the governments in Canada and India have realized the need for accommodating the indigenous communities by granting them greater political autonomy within the bounds of nation states, most indigenous communities in the two countries are now engrossed in debating as to how much political autonomy they should demand and how this could best be put to use to ensure protection and promotion of the interests of the native communities. In Canada the First Nations are unanimous about the need to dispense with the band governments conceived by the Indian Act. Earlier, even the Sechelt Indian Self-Government Act in 1986 was criticized as a demeaning compromise since they felt that what the Act guaranteed to the Sechelt was only a municipal form of government, subordinated to the provincial government. But to this day clear consensus on the structure and form of Indian self-governments has not emerged. Intense debates are taking place within the aboriginal communities on subjects relating to the structure and functioning of the self-governments, their relations with the provincial and Canadian governments, internal resource mobilization, indigenous development strategies, and concern about accountability. As the discussions are still on, the FN organizations have already started making different experiments toward making self-governments relevant to the needs and concerns of the FN communities.[10]

Similarly, several alternative forms of aboriginal self-governments have been proposed and experimented with in the hills of northeast India. The Constitution of India proposed creation of ADCs and ARCs in the hill districts of composite Assam to satisfy the aspirations and concerns of the indigenous communities. While the Nagas refused the offer right at the beginning and demanded independence, other hill communities chose to experiment with the new constitutional arrangements. But in course of time some hill communities began to feel that ADCs did not guarantee protection to tribal identities and interests as they were subordinate to the state government. Therefore, they fought for greater autonomy and some among them could manage to secure state status for the territories they inhabit. These states are often referred to as "tribal states" because of the special privileges they enjoy. Most legislators, ministers and officials running the state governments come from indigenous tribal communities.[11] These state governments have enacted laws seeking protection of tribal lands. Non-tribal communities can neither buy lands nor undertake business in these states without the consent of the state governments or district councils operating in these areas. Special concessions in the form of reservations are made for the education and employment of the indigenous tribal communities. In spite of such immunities some critics have pointed out that these states are not structurally different from other states in the Indian Union. They mobilize few resources from within and are financially dependent on central assistance for running their governments. Most of the policies and schemes they implement are sponsored by the central government. The tribal leaders wielding political power at state or district levels have failed to come out with viable and comprehensive models of development appropriate to the needs of the indigenous peoples. Although the formation of ADCs and "tribal states" could meet the aspirations of the upcoming middle classes to some extent the working of the tribal-led governments in the hills shows that they could not make a qualitative difference to the majority of the tribal people living in the villages with meager means. Further, as critics point out, introduction of formal state structures and practices have weakened community ownership and accentuated class differences within traditional societies, depriving the poor of access to land and forests.[12] On different occasions even insurgent leaders have pointed out these maladies to justify their stand that the indigenous peoples have no future within the Indian Union. Unfortunately, what even the insurgent organizations appear to aspire for as an alternative is to create sovereign states of their own akin to the Indian state. They don't seem to have a clear idea as to how mere secession from the Indian Union or creation of new "tribal states" within the Indian Union would make things better for the indigenous peoples when they do not have any viable alternative vision of a more humane and just society.

Given such not-so-encouraging experiences of the hill communities in northeast India, can one expect a better future for the First Nations, which are presently engaged in negotiations with the federal and provincial governments in Canada for realizing Indian self-government? At one extreme there are a few conservative critics in Canada who predicted the failure of Indian self-governments even before they have become reality. According to them there is no future for aboriginal communities outside the capitalist framework.[13] On the other extreme there are socialists and communists who look at indigenous communities as suppressed and exploited nationalities and argue that genuine self-determination of small nations is possible only when they become part of the working class movement against capitalism and achieve socialism.[14] Against these two positions there are scholars and activists who believe that responsible indigenous self-governments are achievable within the bounds of the Canadian polity, provided the Canadian state gives up its colonial attitude and ensures adequate land and other resources necessary to sustain them.[15]

Some recent developments in Canada appear to strengthen such optimism, the first being that the Canadian government has in principle accepted FNs as First Nations and declared its intention to negotiate honorable treaties with them. Other than advising the First Nations to abide by principles of transparency and accountability the Canadian state is not openly advocating any particular form of Indian self-government. FN communities have wide options open to them to choose an appropriate form of self-government keeping in view their particular history, interests, and aspirations. Going by this trend one can see the possibility of different forms of Indian self-government coming into existence in Canada. The other premise that raises some hopes of successful Indian self-government in Canada is that the scholars and activists sympathetic to the cause of FNs in Canada have been seriously debating questions of considerable relevance to self-government. In what ways should Indian self-government be different from band governments? What should be done to make the Indian leadership accountable to their people? How can Indian governments really become autonomous and self-reliant? Where does the future of FNs' lie, in urban areas or on reserves? Should FNs continue to depend on forests and seas, or explore new avenues for their growth and development? What should native governments do to mobilize internal resources and, what kind of relations should Indian self-governments have with federal and provincial governments?

While exploring answers to such questions many FN communities have also started experimenting with different alternatives with different degrees of success. At this stage of transition it is rather premature to predict how Indian self-governments in Canada are going to shape up and what experiments succeed or fail. But the fact that the right questions are being addressed and debated and different alternatives explored and experimented by the First Nations themselves make one believe that Indian self-governments in Canada will have more indigenous components than what countries like India have at the moment. However, only the coming decades will be able to say for sure whether the indigenous experiments in Canada could come out with viable alternatives to the capitalist–colonial model of development or whether they only facilitate the indigenous peoples' assimilation into the liberal mainstream in a circuitous way. Whatever might be the outcome the indigenous peoples and the governments there in Canada, India will have something new and relevant to learn from the Canadian experience.

Notes and References

1. Some relevant literature on the indigenous worldview in Canada and India includes Marie Smallface Marule, "Traditional Indian Government: Of the People, by the People, for the People," in *Pathways to Self-Determination: Canadian Indians and the Canadian State*, ed. Leroy Little Bear, Menno Boldt and J. Anthony Long (Toronto: University of Toronto Press, 1984), 36–7; Tim Schouls, John Olthuis and Diane Engelstad, "The Basic Dilemma: Sovereignty or Assimilation," in *Nation to Nation: Aboriginal Sovereignty and the Future of Canada*, ed. Diane Engelstad and John Bird (Anansi: Concord, 1992), 14–18; Arbind Kumar, "Tribal Participation", *Seminar*, 514 (2002), http://www.india-seminar.com/2002/514/514%20arbind%20kumar.htm accessed 20 October 2008; Henryk Skolimowski, "Early Tribal Philosophers from Tribal People: Letter from India," *Trumpeter* (1993), http://trumpeter.athabascau.ca/index.php/trumpet/article/viewFile/357/561 accessed 23 October 2008; Sujata Miri, *Khasi World View: A Conceptual Exploration* (Chandigarh: Center for Research for Rural and Industrial Development, 1988).
2. According to the 1991 Census, the tribal population in Arunachal Pradesh was 550,351, in Meghalaya 1,517,927, in Mizoram 653,567 and in Nagaland 1,060,822. The tribal population in the two hill districts of Assam, namely, Karbi-Anglong and North Cachar Hills was 341,718 and 98,834 respectively.
3. Melvin Smith, "Aboriginal Land claims in BC: Serious Concerns about the Nisga'a Deal," *Public Policy Sources*, 16 (Vancouver: Fraser Institute, 1999), http://www.fraserinstitute.org/Commerce.Web/product_files/Nisgaa(v8).pdf accessed 23 February 2008.
4. For more details, see Ch. 2.
5. See Ch. 3.

6. Julia V. Emberley, *Cultural Politics and Decolonization in Canada* (Toronto: University of Toronto Press, 2007), 45–62; John Webster Grant, *Moon of Wintertime: Missionaries and the Indians of Canada in Encounter since 1534* (Toronto: University of Toronto Press, 1984); Kevin Annett, *Hidden from History: The Canadian Holocaust* (Nanaimo: Truth Commission into Genocide in Canada, Nanaimo, 2001).

7. H. Srikanth, "Understanding Ethnic Conflict in Northeast India," in *Ethnicity and Polity in South Asia*, ed. Girin Phukan (New Delhi: South Asian Publishers, 2002), 195–207.

8. See *Gathering Strength: Canada's Aboriginal Action Plan* (Ottawa: DIAND, 1997), 4; Dean Salter, "Twenty Years Beyond the Apology: A Timeline of United Church: First Nations History Since 1986," *Mandate* Special Edition (May 2005), http://www.united-hurch.ca/files/sales/magazines/mandate/2005/may/pdf/0810.pdf accessed 23 February 2008; also Presbyterian Church of Canada, "An Apology to the Aboriginal Peoples of Canada," Indians.org website, http://www.indians.org/welker/apology.htm accessed 23 February 2008.

9. See Expressindia.com (28 October 2003), http://www.expressin-dia.com/news/fullstory.php?newsid=25672 accessed 24 July 2008).

10. For more details, see Ch. 4.

11. In Arunachal Pradesh and Nagaland 59 seats out of 60, 39 out of 40 seats in Mizoram and 55 out of 60 in Meghalaya are reserved for indigenous tribal communities in the state assemblies.

12. See Ch. 5.

13. Tom Flanagan, *First Nations? Second Thoughts* (Toronto: McGill-Queen's University Press, 2000), 189–90.

14. Dick Fidler, *Red Power in Canada* (Toronto: Vanguard Publications, 1970); Central Committee, Communist Party of Canada, "Where Will We Be in Seven Generations?" Central Okanagon Club Resource Centre (21 June 2004), http://cpc.starvingmind.com/_Where_will_we_be_in_Seven_Generations_.shtml accessed 23 February 2008).

15. Alain Cairns, *Citizens Plus: Aboriginal Peoples' and the Canadian State* (Vancouver: University of British Columbia Press, 2002), 177–231; Michael Asch, *Home and Native Land: Aboriginal Rights and Canadian Constitution* (Toronto: Methuen, 1984), 124–42; Cole Harris, *Making Native Space: Colonialism, Resistance and Reserves in British Columbia* (Vancouver: UBC Press, 2002), 293–323.

H. SRIKANTH

SELECT READINGS

Primary Sources

Bhanage, N.P. *Tribal Commissions and Committees in India*. Bombay: Himalaya Publishing House, 1993.

BC Treaty Commission. "Why Treaties?: A Legal Perspective." http://www.bctreaty.net/files/pdf_documents/why_treaties.pdf.

BC Treaty Commission. "Treaties are Good for the Economy." http://www.bctreaty.net/files/economiced1.php.

BC Treaty Commission. "Looking Back Looking Forward: A Review of the BC Treaty Process." http://www.bctreaty.net/files_2/pdf_documents/review_bc_treaty_process.pdf

First Nations Summit. "Framework for Recognition and Reconciliation, Presented to Premier Campbell & Members of British Columbia Cabinet." September 17, 2003. http://www.citizensassembly.bc.ca/resources/submissions/csharman-10_0402271643-470.pdf

Government of British Columbia. "Quick Facts", BC Stats website. http://www.bcstats.gov.bc.ca/data/bcfacts.asp.

Government of British Columbia. *British Columbia: Statistical Profile of Aboriginal Peoples 2001.* Census of Canada 2001. http://www.bcstats.gov.bc.ca/data/cen01/abor/tot_abo.pdf.

Government of Canada. *Gathering Strength - Canada's Aboriginal Action Plan.* Ottawa: Indian and Northern Affairs Canada, 1997.

Government of Canada. *Socio-Economic Indicators in Indian Reserves and Comparable Communities, 1971-1991.* Ottawa: DIAND, 1997.

Government of Canada, *Basic Departmental Data 2003.* Ottawa: DIAND, March 2004.

Government of India, "List of Scheduled Tribes in Census of India 2001", Office of the Registrar General & Census Commissioner website. http://www.censusindia.gov.in/Tables_Published/SCST/scst_main.html.

Government of India, Planning Commission. *Tenth Five Year Plan 2002-07*, Vol.2, Chapter 4.2. http://planningcommission.nic.in/plans/planrel/fiveyr/10th/volume2/v2_ch4_2.pdf.

Government of India, *Basic Statistics of North Eastern Region 2002*, Shillong: North Eastern Council, 2002.

Government of India. *State of Forest Report – 1999.*
Dehradun: Forest Survey of India, 1999.

Government of India, *Report of the Steering Committee on Empowering the Scheduled Tribes for 10th Five Year Plan.*
New Delhi: Planning Commission, 2001. http://planningcommission.nic.in/aboutus/committee/strgrp/stg_st
s.pdf.

Government of India, Ministry of Tribal Affairs, *Annual Report 2004-05.* http://tribal.nic.in/aneng0405.pdf

Government of India. *A Consultation Paper on Empowering and Strengthening of Panchayati Raj Institutions/ Autonomous District Councils/ Traditional Tribal Governing Institutions in North East India.* New Delhi: National Commission to Review the Working of the Constitution, 2001.

Hansaria, Vijay. *Sixth Schedule to the Constitution.* New Delhi: Universal Law Publishing Co., 2005.

Louis, Prakash, ed. *Policy Documents of the Government of India, Compendium I.* New Delhi: Indian Social Institute, 2004.

Louis, Prakash, ed. *Policy Documents of the Government of India, Compendium II.* New Delhi: Indian Social Institute, 2006.

Report of the Survey of Alienation of Tribal Land in Assam. Guwahati: Assam Institute of Research on Tribals and Scheduled Castes, 1999.

Royal Commission on Aboriginal Peoples. *From Public Policy and Aboriginal Peoples 1965-1992*, Vol. 2. Ottawa: RCAP, 1994.

Royal Commission on Aboriginal Peoples. *People to People, Nation to Nation: Highlights from the Report of the Royal Commission on Aboriginal People*. Ottawa: Library and Archives Canada, 1996.

Savyasaachi. *Tribal Forest-Dwellers and Self-Rule -The Constitutional Assembly Debates on the Fifth and Sixth Schedules*. New Delhi: Indian Social Institute, 1998.

The Royal Proclamation of October 7, 1763. Virtual Law Office website. http://www.bloorstreet.com/200block/rp1763.htm.

World Bank, "World Bank Indigenous Peoples' Operational Directive DD 4.2." July 2005.

Secondary Sources

Abele, Frances and Michael J. Prince. "Aboriginal Governance and Canadian Federalism: A To-Do List for Canada." In *New Trends in Canadian Federalism*, edited by Francois Rocher and Miriam Smith. Toronto: Broadway Press, 2003.

Asch, Michael. "Aboriginal Self-Government and Canadian Constitutional Identity: Building Reconciliation." In *Ethnicity and Aboriginality: Case Studies in Ethno-Nationalism*, edited by Michael D. Levin. Toronto: University of Toronto Press, 1983.

Barooah, N.K. *David Scott in North-East India: A Study in British Paternalism*. New Delhi: Munshiram Manoharlal, 1970.

Barpujari H.K., ed. *The Comprehensive History of Assam* Vol. 5. Guwahati: Publication Board Assam, 1993.

——————. *Problem of the Hill Tribes North East Frontier* Vol. I. Shillong: North-Eastern University Publications, 1998.

——————. *Problem of the Hill Tribes North East Frontier* Vol. II. Shillong: North-Eastern Hill University Publications, 1998.

Barua, A.K. *Social Tensions in Assam: Middle Class Politics*. Guwahati: Purbanchal, 1991

——————. "Tribal Traditions and Crises of Governance in North East India with special reference to Meghalaya." Crises States Program, Working Paper no. 22. London: London School of Economics, March 2003. http://www.crisisstates.com/download/wp/WP22AB.pdf.

——————. "Ethnic Conflicts and Traditional Self-Governing Institutions: A Study of Laitumukhrah Dorbar". Crisis States Program, Working Paper no. 39. London: London School of Economics, January 2004. http://www.crisisstates.com/download/wp/wp39.pdf.

Baruah, Sanjib. *India against Itself: Assam and the Politics of Identity*. New Delhi: Oxford University Press, 2001.

————. *Durable Disorder: Understanding the Politics of North-East India.* New Delhi: Oxford University Press, 2005.

Bateman, Rebecca. "Comparative Thoughts on the Politics of Accommodation." *BC Studies: The British Columbia Quarterly*, no. 114, (Summer 1997): 68-78.

Berger, Thomas R. "Native History, Native Claims and Self-determination." *BC Studies*, Special Issue, no. 57, (Spring 1983): 10-23.

Bhattacharjee, J.B. *The Garos and the English 1865-1874.* New Delhi: Radiant Publishers, 1978.

————. *Social and Political Formation: Pre-colonial North East India.* New Delhi: Har-Anand Publications, 1991.

Bhagawati, Dhiren. "Meghalaya the Struggle of the Three Sisters to Have a Place in the Sun." In *Political Dynamics of Northeast India*, edited by Girin Phukon, 175-186. New Delhi: South Asian Publishers, 2000.

Bedford, David. "Marxism and the Aboriginal Question: The Tragedy of Progress." *The Canadian Journal of Native Studies* 14, no. 1, (1994): 101-116.

Beteille, Andre. "The Definition of Tribe." In *Tribe, Caste and Religion in India*, edited by Romesh Thapar, 7-14. Delhi: McMillan, 1977.

————. "The Idea of Indigenous People." *Current Anthropology* 39, no. 2 (1998):187-91.

Bhaumik, Subir. "The Dam and the Tribal." *Himal South Asian*. May, 2004. http://www.himalmag.com/2004/may/perspective.htm.

Boldt, Menno. *Surviving as Indians: The Challenge of Self-Government*. Toronto: University of Toronto Press, 1993.

Bordoloi, B.N. *Transfer and Alienation of Tribal Land in Assam with special reference to the Karbis of the Karbi Anglong District*. Guwahati: Western Book Depot, 1991.

Borrows, John. "Re-Living the Present: Title, Treaties and Trickster in British Columbia." *BC Studies: The British Columbia Quarterly*, no. 120, (Winter 98-99): 99-108.

Cairns, Alain C and Tom Flanagan. "An Exchange." *Inroads*, (September 2001): 42-53. http://www.irpp.org/po/archive/sep01/tf-ac.pdf.

Cairns, Alain C. *Citizens Plus: Aboriginal Peoples' and the Canadian State*. Vancouver: University of British Columbia Press, 2002.

Cassidy, Frank and Robert L. Bish. *Indian Government: Its Meaning in Practice*. Lantz Ville, BC: Oolichan Books and the Institute for Research on Public Policy, 1989.

Champagne, Dune, ed. *Native Americans: Portrait of the People*. Detroit: Visible Inc. Press, 1994.

Changkiri, L. Atola. *The Angami Nagas and the British 1832-1947*. New Delhi: Spectrum Publications, 1999.

Chaubey, S.K. *Hill Politics in Northeast India*. New Delhi: Orient Longman, 1999.

Chaudhury, Buddhadeb. *Tribal Development in India: Problems and Prospects*. New Delhi: Inter-India Publications, 1990.

Chowdhury, J.N. *Arunachal Pradesh: From Frontier Tracts to Union Territory*. New Delhi: Cosmo Publications, 1983.

Coates, Ken S. *Best Left as Indians: Native-White Relations in the Yukon Territory 1840-1973*. Montreal: McGill Queen's University Press, 1991.

Craig, Donna. *Indigenous Peoples and Governance Structures: A Comparative Analysis of Land and Resource Management Rights*. Canberra: Aboriginal Studies Press, 2002.

Creighton, D.G. "The United States and Canadian Confederation." In *Readings in Canadian History: Pre-Confederation*, edited by Douglas Francis and Donald B. Smith, 461-471. Toronto: Holt, Rinehart and Winston of Canada Ltd., 1986.

Das, Debojyoti. "Demystifying the Myth of Shifting Cultivation Agronomy in the North-East." *Economic and Political Weekly* 41, no. 46, November 5, (2006): 4912-4917.

Dash, N.K. "Agrarian Structure and Change in Nagaland." In *Economies of the Tribes and Their Transition*, edited by K.S. Singh, 314-318. New Delhi: Concept Publishing Company, 1982.

Datta Ray, B. *The Emergence and Role of Middle Class in North-East India*. Delhi: Uppal, 1983.

Delgamuukw: The Supreme Court of Canada Decision on Aboriginal Title. Vancouver: Greystone Books, 1998.

Dena, Lal. *Christian Missions and Colonialism: A Study of Missionary Movement in North East India with particular reference to Manipur and Lushai Hills 1894-1947*. Shillong: Vendrame Institute, 1988.

Dupius, Renee. *Justice for Canada's Aboriginal Peoples*. Toronto: James Lorimer and Company Ltd, 2002.

Dyck, Noel, ed. *Indigenous People and the Nation State: Fourth World Politics in Canada, Australia and New Zealand*. St. Johns, Newfoundland: Institute of Social and Economic Research, 1985.

———. *What is the Indian 'Problem': Tutelage and Resistance in Canadian Indian Administration*. Newfoundland: Institute of Social and Economic Research, 1991.

Dyck, Rand. *Canadian Politics: Critical Perspectives*. Nelson: Laurentian University, 2000.

Elwin, Verrier. *A Philosophy for NEFA*. Shillong: NEFA Administration, 1959.

————. "Issues In Tribal Policy Making." In *Tribe, Caste and Religion in India*, edited by Romesh Thapar, 29-37. Delhi: McMillan, 1977.

————. *The Baiga*, Delhi: Gian Publications, 1991edn.

————. *The Tribal World of Verrier Elwin: An Autobiography*, New Delhi: Oxford University Press, 1998.

Ferguson, Niall. *Empire: How Britain Made the Modern World*. London: Penguin, 2002.

Fernandes, Walter, ed. *National Development and Tribal Deprivation*. New Delhi: Indian Social Institute, 1992.

————. "Development Displaced and the Right to Life: Implications for the Northeast." In *Problems of Internally Displaced Persons in Assam with Special Reference to Barak Valley*, edited by Tanmoy Bhattacharjee. Silchar: Assam University, 2003.

First Nations in Canada. Ottawa: Indian and Northern Affairs Canada, 2001.

Fisher, Robin. *Contact and Conflicts: Indian-European Relations in British Columbia, 1774-1890*. Vancouver: UBC Press, 1992.

Flanagan, Tom. *First Nations? Second Thoughts*. Toronto: McGill-Queen's University Press. Toronto, 2000.

Fleras, Augie and Jean L. Elliott. *The Nations Within: Aboriginal-State Relations in Canada, the United States and New Zealand*. Toronto: Oxford University Press, 1992.

H. SRIKANTH

————. *Unequal Relations: An Introduction to Race and Ethnic Dynamics in Canada*. Toronto: Prentice Hall, 2002.

Francis, Douglas and Donald D. Smith, eds. *Readings in Canadian History: Pre-Confederation*. Toronto: Holt, Rinehart and Winston of Canada Ltd., 1986.

Francis, Mark. "The "Civilizing" of Indigenous People in Nineteenth-Century Canada." *Journal of World History* 9, no.1 (1998): 51-87.

Francis, R. Douglas and Donald R. Smith, eds. *Readings in Canadian History: Pre-Confederation*. Ottawa: Holt, Rinehart and Winston of Canada Ltd., 1986.

Frideres, James S. *Native People in Canada: Contemporary Conflicts*. Ontario: Prentice-Hall Canada Inc., 1983.

Gait, Edward. *A History of Assam*. Guwahati: Lawyer's Book Stall, 1992.

Gassah, L.S. "Traditional System of Governance among the Khasis, Jaintias and Garos of Meghalaya and the Changes thereof." In *Polity and Economy: Agenda for Contemporary North East India*, edited by C. Joshua Thomas, 82-89. New Delhi: Regency Publications, 2005.

Ghate, Rucha S. *Forest Policy and Tribal Development: A Study of Maharashtra*, Concept Publishing Company, New Delhi, 1992.

Ghurye, G. S. *The Aborigines So-called and Their Future*. Poona: Gokhale Institute of Politics and Economics, 1943.

————. *The Burning Caldron of North-East India*. Bombay: Popular Prakashan, 1980.

Guha, Ramachandra, *Savaging the Civilized: Verrier Elwin, His Tribals and India*. Chicago: Chicago University Press, 1999.

Getty, Ian and Antoina Lussier. *As Long as the Sun Shines and the Water Flows*. Vancouver: UBC Press, 1983.

Giri, Helen. *The Khasis under British Rule*. New Delhi: Regency Publications, 1998.

Gohain, Hiren. "An Example from Nagaland." *The Assam Tribune*, Guwahati, December 2007. http://www.assamtribune.com/scripts/details.asp?id=dec2007/edit2.

Goswami, Atul, ed. *Traditional Self-government Institutions among Hill Tribes of North East India*. Delhi: Akanksha Publishing House, 2002.

Gough, Barry M "The Character of the British Columbia Frontier." *BC Studies* 32 (Winter, 1976-77): 28-40.

Green, L.C. "Aboriginal Peoples, International Law and the Canadian Charter of Rights and Freedoms." *The Canadian Bar Review*, no. 61, (1983): 339-353.

Habib, Irfan. *Essays in Indian History: Towards a Marxist Perception*. New Delhi: Tulika, 1995.

Harris, Cole. *Making Native Space: Colonialism, Resistance and Reserves in British Columbia*. Vancouver: UBC Press, 2002.

Hasan, Amir. *Tribal Administration in India*. New Delhi: B.R.Publishing House, 1988.

Havemann, P., ed. *Indigenous Peoples' Rights in Australia, Canada and New Zealand*. Auckland: Oxford University Press, 1999.

Hawthorn, H.B. and C.S. Belshow, *The Indians of British Columbia: A Study of Contemporary Social Adjustment*. Toronto: University of Toronto, 1958.

Hemadri, Ravi. "Dams, Displacement, Policy and Law in India", The World Commission on Dams website, http://www.dams.org/docs/kbase/contrib/soc213.pdf.

Isaac, Thomas. "Balancing rights: The Supreme Court of Canada, R.v. Sparrow, and the Future of Aboriginal Rights." *The Canadian Journal of Native Studies* 13, no. 2, (1993): 199-216.

Ivison, Duncan, Paul Patton and Will Sanders, eds. *The Political Theory of Indigenous Peoples* Cambridge: Cambridge University Press, 2000.

Jaimes, Annette M. *The State of Native America: Genocide, Colonization, and Resistance*. Boston: South End Press, 1992.

Jain, Prakash Chandra. *Social Movements among Tribals*. Jaipur: Rawat, 1994.

Jenness, Diamond. *The Indians of Canada*. Toronto: University of Toronto Press, 1993.

Joseph, Shirley. "Assimilation Tools: Then and Now." *BC Studies*, no. 89, (Spring 1991): 65-78

Kar, P.C. *The Garos in Transition*. New Delhi: Cosmo Publications, 1983.

Karlsson, Bengst. "Sovereignty through Indigenous Governance: Reviving 'Traditional Political Institutions' in Northeast India." *The NEHU Journal* 3, no. 2, (2005): 1-15.

Kothari, Ashish. "The Khonoma Magic: A Nagaland Village Leads the Way". Kalpavriksh Environment Action Group website, March 2005. http://www.kalpavriksh.org/f3/regnagaland/Khonoma%20for%20Hindu%20Survey%20final%2012.3.2005.doc.

Kulkarni, Sharad. "The Plight of the Tribal." *Seminar*, no. 492, (2000). http://www.india-seminar.com/2000/492/492%20s.%20kulkarni.htm.

Long, Anthony J. and Menno Boldt, eds. *Governments in Conflict?: Provinces and Indian Nations in Canada*. Toronto: University of Toronto Press, 1988.

Long, Anthony J., Leroy Little Bear and Menno Boldt, eds. *Pathways to Self-Determination: Canadian Indians and the Canadian State*. Toronto: University of Toronto Press, 1984.

Lyngdoh, R. S. *Government and Politics in Meghalaya.*
New Delhi: Sanchar Publishing House, 1996.

Mackenzie, Alexander. *The North-East Frontier of India.*
New Delhi: Mittal Publications, 1994.

Mahapatra, Richnel "At NE Cost: Power for All,
Provider Largely Northeast." *Down to Earth* 12, no. 9,
September 30, (2003).

McInnis, Edgar. *Canada: A Political and Social History.*
Toronto: Holt, Rinehart and Winston of Canada Ltd.,
1961.

McMillan, Allan D. *Native Peoples and Cultures of
Canada: An Anthropological Overview.* Vancouver: Douglas & McIntyre, 1988.

McMillan, Alan D. *Since the Time of the Transformers: The
Ancient Heritage of the Nuu-Chah-Nulth, Ditidaht, and
Makah.* Vancouver, UBC Press, 1999.

McMillan, Allan D and Eldon Yellowhorn. *First Peoples
in Canada.* Vancouver: Douglas McIntyre, 2004.

Miller, Bruce G. *Invisible Indigenes: Politics of Non-recogni-
tion.* Lincoln: University of Nebraska Press, 2003.

Miller, J.R. *Skyscrapers Hide the Heavens: A History of Indian-White Relations in Canada.* Vancouver: UBC Press,
Vancouver, 2002.

Mishra, S.N. *Antiquity to Modernity in Tribal India: Own-ership and Control of Resources among Indian Tribes, Vol. 3.* New Delhi: Inter-India Publications, 1998.

Misra, Udayon. *Periphery Strikes Back: Challenges to the Nation-state in Assam and Nagaland: Challenges to the Na-tion-state in Assam and Nagaland.* Shimla: Institute of Ad-vanced Studies, 2000.

Muckle, Robert J. *The First Nations of British Columbia: An Anthropological Survey.* Vancouver: UBC Press, 1998.

Nag, Sajal. *Contesting Marginality: Ethnicity, Insurgency and Subnationalism in North East India.* Delhi: Manohar, 2002.

Nichols, Roger L. *Indians in the United States & Canada:, A Comparative History.* Lincoln: University of Nebraska Press, 1998.

Nongbri, Tiplut. "Timber Ban in North-East India: Ef-fects on Livelihood and Gender." *Economic and Political Weekly* 36, no. 21, May 26, (2001): 1893-1900.

Nongbri, Tiplut. *Development, Ethnicity and Gender.* New Delhi: Rawat Publications, 2003.

Nuh, V.K., ed. *The Naga Chronicle.* New Delhi: Regency Publications, 2000.

Our Native Peoples: Nootka. Victoria: British Columbia Heritage Series 1, 1996.

H. Srikanth

Prasad, R.N. *Autonomous Movements in Mizoram*. Delhi: Vikas Publishing House, 1994.

————. "Sixth Schedule and Working of the District Councils in North-Eastern States." *Dialogue* 6, No. 2, (October-December 2004). http://www.asthabharati.org/Dia_Oct04/prasad.htm.

Ranjan R. and V.P. Upadhyay. "Ecological Problems due to Shifting Cultivation." *Current Science*, no.77, (1999): 1246-1250.

Raghaviah, V. *Tribal Revolts*. Nellore: Andhra Pradesh Adimjati Sevak Sangh, 1971.

Ray, Animesh. *Mizoram*. New Delhi: National Book Trust, 1993.

Ray, Arthur J. "Introduction: Native People in British Columbia." *Native Studies Review* 11, no. 1 (1996): 167-170.

Richards, John. "A New Agenda For Strengthening Canada's Aboriginal Population." *Backgrounder*, no.66, 2003. http://www.cdhowe.org/pdf/backgrounder_66.pdf.

Rocher, Francois and Miriam Smith. *New Trends in Canadian Federalism*. Toronto: Broadway Press, 2003.

Roy Burman, B.K. "UN Declaration and Safeguards for Protection of Rights of Tribal and Indigenous Peoples". In *Aspiring to Be: Tribal/Indigenous Condition*, edited by Roy Burman, B.K., B.G. Verghese. New Delhi: Konark Publishers Pvt. Ltd., 1988.

————. "Integrated Area Approach to the Problems of the Hill Tribes of North-east India." In *The Tribal Situation in India*, edited by K.S. Suresh Singh, Shimla: IIAS, 1990.

————. "Sixth Schedule of the Constitution." In *Autonomous District Councils*, edited by L.S. Gassah. New Delhi: Omsons Publications, 1997.

————. "Constitutional Framework for Tribal Autonomy with special reference to North-East India." In *North-East India: The Human Interface*, edited by M.K. Raha and Aloke Kumar Ghosh. New Delhi: Gyan Publishing House, 1998.

————. "Indigenous and Tribal Peoples in World System Perspective." *Studies of Tribes and Tribals* 1, no.1, (July 2003): 7-27.

Sabhawal Y.K. Address to the Pleanary Session of International Law Association in Toronto. http://www.supremecourtofindia.nic.in/new_links/ILA-TORONTO.doc.

Salter, Dean. "Twenty Years beyond the Apology: A Timeline of United Church – First Nations History since 1986." Mandate Special Edition, May 2005. http://www.united-church.ca/files/sales/magazines/mandate/2005/may/pdf/0810.pdf.

Sarma, S. "Shifting cultivation in Meghalaya." *North East-ern Geographer*, no. 19, (1987): 61-69.

Satzewich, Wotherspoon. *First Nations: Race, Class and Gender Relations.* Scarborough: Nelson Canada, 1993.

Saxena, Naresh C. "National Draft Policy on Tribals: Suggestions for Improvement." National Advisory Council, Government of India. http://nac.nic.in/concept%20papers/draft_goi_tribal.pdf.

Sema, Piketo. *British Policy and Administration in Naga-land 1881-1947.* New Delhi, Scholar Publishing House, 1992.

Sharma, B.D. "Reassertion by the Community in the Tribal Areas." *Dialogue* 3, no.2, (October-December, 2001).

————. *Taming the Transition in Scheduled Areas.* Delhi: Sahyog Pustak Kutir, 2001.

Sheperd, Robert and Russel Diabo, "A Government-First Nations Dialogue on Accountability: Reestablishing Un-derstanding on the Basics of a Complex Relationship." *Native Studies Review* 15, no. 2, (2004): 61-81.

Singh A.K. and M.K. Jabbi, eds. *Tribals in India: Develop-ment, Deprivation, Discontent.* New Delhi: Har-Anand, 1995.

Singh, Bhupinder. "Perspective and Plans." In *Socio-economic and Ecological Development*, edited by Bhuddadeb Chaudhuri. New Delhi: Inter-India Publications, 1992.

————. *Antiquity to Modernity in Tribal India – Tribal Self-management in North-East India, Vol. 2*. New Delhi: Inter-India Publications, 1998.

Singh, K.S. *Tribal Movements in India*. New Delhi: Manohar, 1982.

Slowey, Gabriell A. "Aboriginal Self-Government, Extinguishment of Title and the Canadian State: Effectively Removing the "Other?" *Native Studies Review* 13, no. 1, (2000).

Smith, Dan. *The Seventh Fire: The Struggle for Aboriginal Government*. Toronto: Key Porter Books, 1993.

Smith, Melvin. *Our Home or Native Land?: What Government's Aboriginal Policy is Doing to Canada*. Toronto: Stoddart Publishing Co. Limited, 1995.

Snaitang, O.L. *Christianity and Social Change in Northeast India*. Shillong: Vendrame Institute, 1983.

Tennant, Paul. "Native Indian Political Organization in British Columbia, 1900-1969: A Response to Internal Colonialism." *BC Studies*, no. 55, (1981): 26-49.

————. "Native Indian Political Activity in British Columbia, 1969-1983." *BC Studies*, no. 57, Special Issue, (Spring 1983): 112-114.

————. *Aboriginal Peoples and Politics: The Indian Land Question in British Columbia 1849-1989.* Vancouver: UBC Press, 1990.

————. "Aboriginal Peoples and Aboriginal Title in British Columbia Politics." In *Politics, Policy and Government in British Columbia*, edited by R.K. Carty. Vancouver: UBC Press, 1996.

Thornton, A.P. *Doctrines of Imperialism.* New York: John Wiley and Sons, 1965.

Venkat Rao, V. *Tribal Politics in North East India 1874-1974.* Delhi: S. Chand and Company, 1976.

Verghese, B.G. "The Bounty of North-Eastern Waters." In *Challenges of Development in North-East India*, edited by Anuradha Datta, David R. Syiemlieh and Srinath Barua, 192-207. New Delhi: Regency Publications, 2006.

Von Furer Haimendorf, Christopher. "Aboriginal Rebellions in Deccan." *Man in India* 25, no. 4, (December 1945): 208-216.

Weaver, Sally W. *Making Canadian Indian Policy: The Hidden Agenda 1968-70.* Toronto: University of Toronto Press.

Wherrett, Jill. Aboriginal Self-Government. Ottawa: Library of Parliament, 1996.

Xaxa, Virginius. "Tribes as Indigenous People of India." *Economic and Political Weekly*, December 18, (1999): 3589-3596.

————. "Positive Discrimination: Why Scheduled Tribes Lag Behind Scheduled Castes?" *Economic and Political Weekly*, July 21, 2001, 2766-2772.

H. Srikanth

APPENDIX A

Major First Nations in British Columbia
Beaver (Dunne-za)
Chilcotin (Tsilhqot'in)
Comox
Cree
Dalkelh (Central and Southern Carrier)
Dididaht, Pacheedaht (Nootka)
Gitksan, Nisga'a
Haisla (Northern Kwakiutl)
Halkomelem
Heiltsuk (Bella Bella, Northern Kwakiutl)
Kaska, Dena
Kwakwaka'wakw (Kwakiutl)
Nlaka'pamux (Thompson)
Nuu-chah-nulth (Nootka)
Nuzalk (Bella Coola)
Okanagan
Oweekeno (Northern Kwakiutl)
Sechelt
Secwepemc (Shuswap)
Slavey (Dene-thah)
Squamish
Stl'atl'imx (Lillooet)
Straits Sallish
Tagish
Tahitan
Tsimshian
Tutchone
Wet'suwet'en (Western Carrier)

APPENDIX B

Major Hill Tribes of Composite Assam
(With population over 10,000 as on 1991)

* Adi
* Adi Gallong
* Adi Mayong
* Angami
* Ao
* Aptani
* Bangni
* Chakhasang
* Chakma
* Chang
* Chang
* Dimasa Kachari
* Garo
* Hajong
* Hmar
* Hmar
* Jaintia
* Khasi
* Khiemnungam
* Konyak
* Kuki tribes
* Lakher
* Lotha
* Lushai
* Mikir
* Nishang
* Nissi
* Pawi
* Phom
* Rengma
* Sangtam
* Sema
* Tagin

H. SRIKANTH

* Wancho
* Yimchangr
* Zeliang

APPENDIX C

First Nations Population in Canada 2001

Name of Canadian Province/ Territory	Total Popula- tion	First Nation Population	As % of Total FN Population in Canada	As % of Provincial/ Territorial Population
Newfoundland & Labrador	508,080	7,040	1.16	1.39
Prince Edward Island	133,385	1,035	0.17	0.78
Nova Scotia	897,565	12,920	2.12	1.44
New Brunswick	719,710	11,495	1.89	1.60
Quebec	7,125,580	51,125	8.40	0.72
Ontario	11,285,545	131,560	21.61	1.17
Manitoba	1,103,700	90,340	14.84	8.19
Saskatchewan	963,155	84,745	13.91	8.79
Alberta	2,941,150	84,995	13.96	2.89
British Columbia	3,868,875	118,295	19.43	3.06
Yukon Territory	28,520	5,600	0.92	19.64
Northwest Territory	37,100	10,615	1.74	28.61
Nunavut	26,665	95	0.02	0.36
Canada	29,639,030	608,850	100	2.05

Source: 2001 Census of Population - Statistics Canada.

APPENDIX D

State-wise Scheduled Tribe Populations in India 2001
*Including the population of Union Territories

Name of the State	Population of the State	ST Population of the State	ST Population as % of State Population
Andhra Pradesh	76,210,007	5,024,104	6.6
Arunachal Pradesh	1,097,968	705,158	64.2
Assam	26,655,528	3,308,570	12.4
Bihar	82,998,509	758,351	0.9
Chattisgarh	20,833,803	6,616,596	31.8
Goa	1,347,668	566	0.04
Gujarat	50,671,017	7,481,160	14.8
Haryana	21,144,564	N/A	0.0
Himachal Pradesh	6,077,248	244,587	4.02
Jammu & Kashmir	10,069,917	1,105,979	10.9
Jharkhand	26,945,829	7,087,068	26.3
Karnataka	52,850,562	3,463,986	6.6
Kerala	31,838,619	364,189	1.14
Madhya Pradesh	60,348,023	12,233,474	20.3
Maharashtra	96,878,627	8,577,276	8.9
Meghalaya	2,318,822	1,992,862	85.9
Manipur	2,166,788	741,141	34.2
Mizoram	888,573	839,310	94.5
Nagaland	1,990,036	1,774,026	89.1
Orissa	36,706,920	8,145,081	22.1
Punjab	24,289,296	N/A	0.0
Rajasthan	56,507,188	7,097,706	8.4
Sikkim	540,851	111,405	20.6
Tamilnadu	62,405,679	651,321	1.0
Tripura	3,199,203	993,426	31.1
Uttaranchal	8,489,349	256,129	3.0
Uttarpradesh	166,197,921	107,963	0.1
West Bengal	80,176,197	4,406,794	5.5
India*	**1,027,015,247**	**84,326,240**	**8.21**

Source: Data Highlights: ST Population, Census of India, 2001.

APPENDIX E

Demographic Profile of Aboriginal Peoples in British Columbia, 2001

Category	British Columbia		Canada Total	
	Number	*%*	*Number*	*%*
First Nations	123,785	72.8	632,265	64.76
Metis	44,260	26.0	292,300	29.94
Inuit	805	0.5	45,075	4.62
Multiple Responses	1,175	0.7	6,665	0.68
Total	170,025	100	976,305	100

Source: British Columbia: Statistical Profile of Aboriginal Peoples, Census of Canada, 2001.

APPENDIX F

On- and Off-Reserve Registered First Nation Population in Canada

Year	On-Reserve		Off-Reserve		Total	
	No.	*%*	*No.*	*%*	*No.*	*%*
1982	235,640	70.9	96,538	29.1	332,178	100
1987	268,474	64.6	147,424	35.4	415,898	100
1992	315,663	59.2	217,798	40.8	533,461	100
1997	365,806	58.3	261,629	41.7	627,435	100

Source: Basic Departmental Data 2003, Department of Indian Affairs and Northern Development, March 2004.

APPENDIX G

Representation of STs in Political Decision-Making Institutions: 1995-2001

Category	Total India	Total STs	
		No.	%
Gram Panchayats	2,880,261	235,445	9.1
Panchayat Samitis	128,581	7,237	5.6
Zilla Parishads	13,484	1,170	8.7
State Legislative Assemblies (in 2000)	4,072	530	13.0
Parliament (in 1999)	543	41	7.5

Source: Government of India, Ministry of Tribal Welfare, *Annual Report 2004-05.*

APPENDIX H

Legislative Assembly Seats Reserved for STs in Hill States of Northeast India

Name of the State	Total Seats	Reserved for STs
Arunachal Pradesh	60	59
Meghalaya	60	55
Mizoram	40	39
Nagaland	60	59

Source: Government of India, Election Commission, *Hand Book for Returning Officers.*

APPENDIX I

Representation of STs in Central Government Services: 1974-1999

Category	Group A	Group B	Group C	Group D	Total
As on Jan. 1, 1974					
Total	33,672	52,343	1,566,796	1,242,548	2,895,359
ST Total	155	258	33,383	47,679	81,475
ST %	0.46	0.49	2.13	3.84	2.81
As on Jan. 1, 1994					
Total	59,016	103,198	2,381,613	1,023,285	3,567,112
ST Total	1,727	2,902	128,228	62,945	195,802
ST %	2.92	2.81	5.38	6.15	5.49
As on Jan. 1, 1999					
Total	93,520	104,963	2,396,426	949,353	3,544,262
ST Total	3,172	3,512	145,482	66,487	218,653
ST %	3.39	3.35	6.07	7.0	6.17

Source: Government of India, Ministry of Tribal Welfare, *Annual Report 2004-05.*

H. Srikanth

INDEX

Chutias 62
Citizen-Plus 117
Coast Salish 33, 107
Colonialism iii, 1, 22, 23, 27, 52, 57, 59, 60, 87, 98, 138, 190, 203, 213, 217, 224
Comox 33, 227
Convention No. 169 (see *International Labor Organization*)
Cowichan 33, 107
Cree 119, 227
David Scott 68, 70, 82, 83, 98, 209
David Thompson 30
Dene Declaration 118
Dimasas 63, 65, 154, 188
Dorbars 158, 159, 160
Duflas 62, 70, 80
East India Company 60, 61, 82
First Ministers' Conference 114, 115
Fishing 28, 35, 36, 40, 46, 50, 51, 66, 105, 112, 122, 123, 161, 189
Fort Rupert 40, 45
Frank Calder 107, 111
Frederick Seymour 32
Fur trade 29, 30, 31, 37, 38, 39, 40, 43, 50, 56
Garo Hills District 81
Garos 63, 67, 68, 70, 73, 74, 75, 79, 83, 84, 87, 89, 93, 98, 99, 153, 154, 179, 189, 193, 210, 215, 218
George Vancouver 30
George Walkem 48
Gilbert Sproat 48
Gitksan 33, 132, 227
Gold rush 40
Gonds 14
Gopinath Bordoloi 94
Haida 33, 37
Harold Cardinal 110
Hawthorn Committee 107, 108
    Hawthorn Report 107, 108
HBC (see *Hudson's Bay Company*)
Hill Miris 62
Hmars 63
Hudson's Bay Company v, 19, 31, 32, 40

Hunting 4, 17, 28, 35, 36, 37, 38, 40, 50, 60, 66, 67, 105, 119, 160, 161, 165, 189
Hupasceth 132
Indian Act 13, 49, 50, 52, 54, 101, 102, 103, 104, 105, 108, 109, 113, 116, 119, 120, 121, 126, 137, 197
Inner Line 76, 77, 78, 79, 85, 92, 148
    Inner Line Regulations 76, 77, 78, 85, 92, 148
International Labor Organization v, 3
    Convention No. 169 3
Inuit 9, 11, 115, 131, 188, 195, 231
IPACC v, 4, 23
Jaintia Hills 73, 74, 78, 80, 81, 84, 88, 91, 148, 154
Jaintias 63, 65, 70, 73, 74, 79, 84, 87, 93, 153, 179, 189, 193, 215
James Cook 30, 39
James Douglas 31, 32, 45, 139
Jarawas 14
Jawaharlal Nehru 155
Jhum 160, 161, 163, 164, 174
Joseph Trutch 47
Justice Emmett Hall 111, 112
Karbis 63, 154, 183, 188, 211
Kaska 33, 227
Kebang 158
Khamptis 66, 69, 76
Khamtis 63, 69, 70, 80
Khasi Hills (see *Khasi-Jaintia Hills*)
Khasi Students Union 168
Khasi-Jaintia Hills 73, 74, 78, 80, 83, 84, 88, 91, 94, 148, 154, 169, 171, 172
Khasis 63, 66, 70, 73, 74, 79, 84, 87, 89, 93, 98, 149, 153, 179, 189, 193, 215, 216
Koches 62
Kootenay 33
Kukis 6, 63, 76, 92, 93, 188
Kwakiutl 30, 33, 37, 227
Lakhers 63
Lillooet 30, 33, 227
Lushais 63, 67, 72, 73, 86
Meech Lake Accord 116
Meenas 14

North Cachar Hills 20, 63, 72, 79, 87, 88, 91, 94, 148, 150, 154, 158, 169, 188, 202
North West Company v, 19, 30
Northwest Territories 13, 18, 118, 188, 195
NSCN-IM 8
Nunavut 13, 131, 195, 229
Nuu-Chah-Nulth 12, 41, 56, 107, 113, 135, 219, 227
Oka Crisis 123, 126
Okanagans 37
Okanagon 33, 203
Pawis 63
Penner Committee 116, 117, 121
Posa 67, 72
Potlatch 36, 44, 50, 54, 105
RCAP (see *Royal Commission on Aboriginal Peoples*)
Royal Commission on Aboriginal Peoples v, 124, 125, 138, 208
Salish 33, 37, 107
Salishian 33, 36
Santhals 14
Scheduled District Act 77
Sekani 30, 33, 36, 48
Shuswap 30, 33, 107, 227
Simon Fraser 11, 30, 39
Singphos 63, 66, 68, 69, 70, 73, 76, 80, 85
Slave 33, 36, 37, 48, 67
Socialism 23, 200
Southern Vancouver Island Tribal Federation v, 107
Straits Salish 33
SVITF (see *Southern Vancouver Island Tribal Federation*)
Syiems 66, 74, 81, 94, 158
Tahltan 33
Tangkhul Nagas 63
Terra nullius 111, 122
Thompson River 30, 36
Tlingit 33, 37
Treaty of Paris 29
Tripuris 63
Tsimshian 33, 42, 227
U. Tirot Singh 73
UBCIC (see *Union of British Columbia Indian Chiefs*)

H. Srikanth

www.ingramcontent.com/pod-product-compliance
Lightning Source LLC
Chambersburg PA
CBHW070807270326
41927CB00010B/2339